# Starved For Success

## Powerful Lessons on Resilience and Resourcefulness from an International Entrepreneur

Olivia Ansell

The events and conversations in this book have been set down to the best of the author's ability, although some names and details have been changed to protect the privacy of individuals.

Copyright © Olivia Ansell, 2021

All rights reserved. This book or any portion thereof may not be reproduced or used in any manner whatsoever without the written permission of the author except for the use of brief quotations in a book review.

Book Cover Design by: Chelsea Alphonso

Cover photography by: Erick Robinson

A WritersBlok Production

Printed in the United States of America

First edition, 2021.

Hardcover ISBN 978-1-7369059-0-6

EBook ISBN 978-1-7369059-1-3

# Contents

Introduction .................................................................................. v

**PART I: Growing Pains** ........................................................... 1

Chapter 1: From Riches To Rags ................................................ 2
Chapter 2: Hungry For More .................................................... 27
Chapter 3: Longing For An Illusion .......................................... 55

**PART II: New World View** ...................................................... 87

Chapter 4: Working Girl ............................................................ 88
Chapter 5: A New World ........................................................... 105

**PART III: The American Dream** ............................................. 143

Chapter 6: How To Build An Empire ........................................ 144
Chapter 7: Trouble In Paradise .................................................. 193
Chapter 8: The Bigger Picture .................................................... 246
About Author ............................................................................. 271

# Introduction

## Getting Uncomfortable

I will never forget the moment when I finally realized that my life wouldn't be the same. My mother, sister and I were being kicked out of the only home I ever knew. Forced to live in a cramped storage room by bitter aunties, uncles, and step-siblings, we were given one week to collect our things and leave. And to make sure we left in the given amount of time, they turned off the electricity, which made it extremely difficult to see all of our belongings that were stuffed inside along with us. I was 10 years old, I had just lost my dad, and with his life also went my easy childhood. My dad had been a successful entrepreneur and as is the custom in Uganda, he owned several estates, each home to a wife and children. He took care of everyone in our huge extended family, and even paid rent and bought food for people I'd never met. My dad was the heart of our home. While he was alive, I never felt like there was anything we lacked. Almost instantly everything had completely changed for me the moment I learned about his death.

Throughout my life, I've noticed that every single time I'm faced with an uncomfortable situation, I push myself even harder to get out of it. This is something that has become second nature to me, something I really cannot help. In the first few days after losing my dad, we didn't have anything. We left our lush estate behind for a small shack in the slums where the electricity would go out every day, and when it rained, the whole house would flood for hours. The only thing I remember having was a lingering belly pain from not eating for what would sometimes be days on end. But even then, I knew the hunger I felt ran deeper than just wanting chicken for dinner. I was starved for success – craving a comfortability that would only come once I had enough cash to take care of myself and my family. I knew I needed money, so I went out and did whatever I felt was necessary to get it. As a child growing up in a poor community in Uganda, that meant becoming imaginative with how I helped support us, and eventually starting my first side-hustle before the age of 13.

Now I'm not saying you have to be dirt poor and starving in an under-developed country to start a business. However, I know that experiencing adversity has helped me tremendously in my entrepreneurial journey. Since I was a child, I've pushed myself past what's expected. I even find myself pushing past what most people think is possible.

## Embracing Change

We can't predict what will happen in life or what the future might bring us, but we can prepare ourselves to face the inevitable curve balls. There is a saying in my country that has helped me tremendously throughout the years. Roughly translated, the saying goes, *'there is nothing that doesn't end.'* When you're going through something difficult, there's nothing better than knowing that once the appropriate amount of time passes, then that suffering will too. That aphorism doesn't just apply to the hard moments, but to every single moment we might experience – including the ones we love. In my life, I've learned that those times where we are happy and most comfortable must also come to an end. Although in a process where everything has a final point, it's up to us to make sure that when things do stop, we end up on top.

Once things changed, so did I. I began doing whatever I had to do to make the circumstances work in my favor because I felt like I had no choice. I knew my life was changing, whether positively or negatively, that was ultimately up to me. And if it meant being broke again, then I was already dead-set on not letting that happen. Scaling my businesses to unimaginable levels made me realize how much potential we all have to do extraordinary things once we're faced with change and driven to operate outside of our safety net.

What I've learned since becoming a wife and businesswoman is how important it is to trust my intuition. I've learned a lot through trial and error, and I've fully embraced my infatuation with taking risks. Many busy, working mothers question whether they are doing enough. These are the same women who've put their dreams aside to make space for the ambitions and needs of their husbands and children. It wasn't too long ago when I was faced with the task of deciding whether or not I should put myself first for once in my life. I had hit a challenging point in my marriage, and I asked myself what it was I actually wanted. Life as I knew it had come to a crossroads where my reality of being a stay-at-home mom and the desire to still pursue entrepreneurship collided, and I needed to find a balance to make it all work. For a short moment, I wasn't sure if it was possible to be the powerful woman in business I wanted to be and still take care of my family as the mother and wife they'd known. But what I want you to understand is that no matter how stretched you might feel, you are enough. It is absolutely possible to do the things that seem to be out of the ordinary or untraditional. You just have to trust yourself.

And maybe your dream is not to become a millionaire or to run a business. Perhaps your goal is to finally take that solo trip to Europe or skydive from a plane 15,000 ft in the air. Whatever you hope to achieve, this book is designed to help you do that. Through my life experiences, I've learned that we must continuously work toward bettering ourselves and our surroundings because it's the only way we can make a lasting impact that meaningfully affects our lives. Each of us has no choice but to face change every single day, but it is what we do when faced with these changing circumstances that make all the difference. Maybe a shift in your life has brought you to this book. Maybe you are reading this book right now because you are longing for some kind of confirmation between these pages. Whatever brought you here, you must recognize the power you have to redefine success on your own terms. You are not here by chance. Realize that there's never a reason why you should feel like you have no control over what happens in your life. Embrace change and launch your own life's mission by doing things differently.

## Shifting Perspective

Growing up in Uganda, I felt like there wasn't much for me to aspire to other than becoming a submissive wife to a domineering husband and a doting mother to as many kids that came. And I don't mean to ruffle the feathers of any native Ugandans who may be reading this, but at that time that's what I was used to seeing. As I watched my older sister and female cousins live out married lives that didn't seem at all fulfilling, I couldn't help but be repelled by the idea of willingly accepting that kind of path for myself, so I chose to become a dreamer. Every chance I got, I dreamt of what life would be like once I grew up and moved to a place where I could have my own business, my own money and the means to take care of my entire family. Most nights, I would lie awake with the hot evening air stinging my cheeks, my mother and sister sleeping soundly next to me on the bare floor of our one room home in the slums. Often cuddled up with nothing but a small sheet, I closed my eyes and envisioned an enormous mansion lined end to end with tables filled with all kinds of delicious foods. I remember visualizing the life I wanted, and what I could see in my mind was so much more appetizing than my reality. Even though I was never sure of how I would experience any of the things I dreamt of, I truly believed the difficult time I was facing would eventually end. That's the thing I love about children and often see it in my own kids as I raise them. They understand and wholeheartedly believe in limitless possibIlities. They follow their curiosity and aren't afraid to pursue something, regardless of the risks involved. I hope this book reminds you to reconnect with your childlike wonder. Whether you are a mother or not, we have all experienced a child's innocence. We've seen the future in their eyes. This shift in mindset toward manifestation has never fallen short on me, and because of that shift,

I have created my life and have not allowed someone else to control the narrative.

I believe that each and every one of us has had an idea for a business or invention at some point in our lives, but many of us don't act on those ideas simply because we're afraid. For many of us, we don't feel worthy of success. Others may not believe they're capable of getting there in the first place. Our circumstances might condition us to think that there are things we can't achieve or places we can't ever go. Maybe someone close to you has told you outright to your face that you will never amount to anything. I know exactly how it feels to have people look at you like you're insignificant. Nevertheless, when nobody else believes in you, you have to believe in yourself.

As a child, I embodied an entrepreneurial spirit and didn't even know it. When I started my first hustle, I didn't understand the return on investment. I wasn't worried about supply and demand, and I didn't use a balance sheet. I was drawn to a problem, and I knew I needed to make money as soon as possible. I believed I could earn a small income by starting with just an idea and building on the next practical step. While my father was alive, I was far too young to truly grasp his business acumen, but I can't help but think that since his passing, his hand has guided me throughout the toughest of times.

The truth is, there is no way you will be able to recognize business opportunities if you have not trained your mind to look for them. We all have imaginations, but some of us never use them, and that can make the world seem much more rigid than it actually is. Just think, how often do you find yourself daydreaming? How often do you direct your energy toward something you like, something you find worthwhile instead of something you're having trouble with? In learning about the law of attraction, I've been able to understand that all the energy that we direct toward the things we think about pulls us closer and closer to them until finally, these things can be ours. What is your energy pulling you closer to?

I feel like most people have no problem with losing the sense of wonder that we have as children. Maybe they think it's just a part of growing up, I'm not sure. Our imagination is what gives us the chance to envision our future. With that comes goals to reach, places to go, and new experiences to have. Experiences that are worlds away from where we are now. Believe me when I say that until you begin looking at your life for what it could be instead of just fixating on what is, you will never know anything different.

## Becoming Resilient

I've started too many businesses to count. Each one wasn't always successful, but there was never a time in my life where I made an excuse as to why something did not work out for me. Anytime I've had a failure, I turned my focus around to learn from it. I asked myself hard questions like, *'What could I have done differently? Was there a moment I didn't do enough research before I made a decision? How can I take this loss and turn it into a win?'* Instead of justifying my weaknesses, I leaned more into my strengths. I made myself the sole person responsible for whether I succeeded or not. Because whenever we use our situation as an excuse for failure, we're only hurting ourselves. No one on the face of this earth can keep you from getting up and starting whatever business, project, or adventure you'd like, except for you.

Everything I've achieved has been due to my own business principles that anyone can apply anywhere.
1. Dream beyond your comfort zone
2. Validate your business idea
3. Map out your plan and execute

That's it. I told you it was simple. In my journey as an entrepreneur, I've learned that not a single one of those principles I mentioned costs money, but the time and effort applied to each is what gives them their value. And you might be thinking, *'but how do I do all of those things?'* In this book, you'll learn how to find business ideas for yourself, how to validate those ideas and eventually transform your goals into meaningful returns worthy of building wealth. Now it's your turn to take a chance and act on your skills with the resources you have access to. Once you change your mindset, you'll start identifying opportunities everywhere you look. When you understand how to observe the market and what you can do with that research and data, then you will be able to change your reality. As long as you are moving forward, you are headed in the right direction. But you have to make those moves for yourself. No one else can do it for you. Because having access to all the opportunities in the world means nothing if you don't use them.

# PART I:

## Growing Pains

# CHAPTER 1

# From Riches To Rags

## A lesson on embracing change

Say you bake a cake. And when you do, you use a recipe that you really believe will help you make the best cake you've ever tasted. You have this idea that if you follow the recipe exactly to the tee, it's going to turn out just the way your mother or grandmother used to make it, but in the end, when you take that first bite, you realize there's something missing. The cake smells the same, it looks exactly how it's supposed to look, but it doesn't give you that same satisfying, happy, or nostalgic feeling you might've hoped for. That one special thing that can't be measured, written down on a piece of paper, or even purchased is not there. It's something unshakable and unspoken that can't be articulated with a simple list of ingredients and heating instructions. It can only be felt and understood by us while the baking is in progress, recognized by others only once the dish is finally shared. The thing that can only be translated through the work and felt in the results is missing. Life can be like this. We all have a story, but sometimes what our stories are missing is that one defining event or distinguishing moment that changes the course of our entire lives and leaves an influence on the rest of our days. That thing that makes the story of our life *our* life story, and enables us to lead a distinct existence. For unknown reasons, these things weigh heavy on our hearts and minds, incapable of being scaled but fully unique to each of us as they shape who we become and dictate our experiences.

I am not the first girl who has stories to tell about growing up in the slums of Uganda. I am not the only one who, despite all the odds, made it out to lead a happy and successful life. I am not the only business woman to start and grow several successful enterprises across different industries. And, I am not the only person who, despite having no advanced education, no connections, and no money, strived, worked, and managed to become a multimillionaire before the age of thirty. Rags to riches stories like mine are as old and as numerous as stories themselves. Maybe you've heard or read so many that they all blend together – the same themes, ideas, and advice. Or maybe you're especially interested in mine because you see that it is somehow different. Somehow special. I can't promise that by reading this book you will be taught to become like me. But I do hope it inspires you to put your own spin on life. To change your trajectory if you're not moving where you'd like to go, and lead the life you want rather than the one people insist you were born to lead.

## Something Is Missing

If you are born into a life where you are surrounded by people who keep you safe, and things in your little world are predictable, secure, and stable, you are lucky. But you are also blissfully unaware that everything is resting on something that is anything but solid. Somewhere in the background, there is an invisible clock silently ticking down the remaining minutes of normalcy left in your life. In that final fraction of a second, everything you know, expect, and rely on evaporates from underneath you. It is the moment that you understand how lucky you once were. For the first time, you feel loss. You learn that life is not predictable but precarious, and you get your first introduction to fear and uncertainty. You awaken in the absence of what is no longer there, and you feel driven by desperation to get it all back. It is a defining and life altering moment. For me, that moment started with the sudden and unexpected death of my father. The awakening that took me from safety to uncertainty, security to fear, and stability to desperation stretched over a span of two years as pieces of my former life eroded from beneath me. Before my dad died, I can't say that I was really missing anything. With him in my life, everything I wanted I already had. It wasn't until he was gone that I found one unique thing to my story that continues to set me apart and set me up for success.

As a small child, I lived comfortably with my mom and sister. I remember attending nice boarding schools and having closets full of beautiful dresses. Every day I woke up, did my chores, played outside with my siblings, and tried to stay out of my elders' way. In Africa, adults or elders do not engage with children the way they do in Western cultures. Our job as children was to do the few things they demanded of us and to generally stay out of their way otherwise, which we were happy to do. My home was in a secure and beautiful compound that we shared with extended family, so I was surrounded by people who kept me safe and happy.

The family dynamic in Uganda is much different than most parts of the world. The man is thought of and treated as the head of the household. He makes the decisions, has the power, and holds ultimate control over the people in the home. His word is law, and his family is expected to obey. It is also acceptable for him to have multiple wives if he chooses to do so, and this is not strange or unusual in Ugandan culture. My mother was one of five wives, and my father treated her like a queen. My mother ran our household expertly. I could see even at a very young age that my father trusted her to raise my sister and I properly. She was a good wife to him, and he was a wonderful husband to her and father to us. We loved him dearly.

But with five different families, as you can imagine, we had no choice but to share our dad with my other half siblings. He'd visit us at our family home roughly once a week. Each day I would look forward to my father's weekly visit, thinking that I was one day closer to having him all to myself for a while. To someone who grew up outside of a culture like mine, this might sound strange. Having a father who is not present day in and day out is not an exception in Uganda. It is actually quite common, especially for the exceptionally wealthy. Not having my father there every day made the time that he was there feel like a gift or a holiday. His visits told us that we were important to him and that we mattered. Every visit felt like a celebration. My dad was both a very wealthy man and a very good man. He made sure his wives were taken care of and that we were all comfortable in our own homes. And even though we didn't get much alone time with him, the time he gave was special. I felt loved. When my dad would visit where we lived, I remember my sister and I thought those nights were the best nights of the week. Mostly because he would always give us money to buy extra snacks that we wouldn't normally have at home.

One of the fondest memories I have of my dad was when he met with my sister and I after we'd just come back from boarding school. But to understand this story, you need to know a little bit about something called posho. For those who do not know, posho is made of cornmeal cooked with water to a porridge-like consistency. Overcook it and it's more like a semi-solid wet dough that sits on your plate like a lump. Undercook it and it's a drippy, soupy tasteless mush. Posho is meant to be a side dish served with beef and sauce, but in the absence of meat or for cost savings, beans can be added to boost the nutrition. It is something you can make in large quantities to feed school children and prisoners or if you are poor, something you can scrape together from almost nothing and eat to stay alive. Posho is one of those things that could be good, but generally isn't. It's dull, tasteless, and little more than a kid's best option to going hungry. And posho was all we ever ate at school! As the weeks at boarding school went by, not only did we count down the days until classes would end, but we also counted the number of bowls of posho we had to eat until we were back at home. When that day came, I walked home dreaming and imagining what glorious food would be on the table. Needless to say, the word misery cannot begin to describe our feelings when we came home to find my mother preparing posho for dinner!

We tried to hide our despair, but couldn't completely contain our groaning and whining. That's when we noticed our father was present. Overhearing our complaints about having to eat the same boring meal at school, my father stood up. We were acting disobedient, disrespectful, and ungrateful. I knew it would not be tolerated. But instead of getting angry or punishing us, my father reached into his pocket and handed my sister and I five dollars each. "Here," he said. "Just go buy whatever you want to eat then." My sister and I lit up and clutched those dollars like they were a lost treasure and our last possession. Giving five dollars back then to young girls like us was almost like saying, *'Okay, here's a hundred bucks for you and a hundred bucks for you.'* We couldn't believe that we had that much money to ourselves. I remember my mom being so upset. She glared at my dad, probably thinking to herself, *'Why would you give them that much money?'* It was one of those glares I've given my own husband a hundred times. Generally it's because he does something like let our children have cookies for breakfast. But that was the kind of person my father was. He was generous, thoughtful, and kind.

At this point, sometimes it's a little difficult for me to remember exactly how he was or what he looked like, but I'll never forget how special my father made me feel. He was tall and kind of quiet. He wasn't someone who yelled or had to raise their voice for people to pay attention. As a child, good behavior is expected at all times. In most places in Africa, we're raised like that; to be respectful. When I was growing up, good behavior looked like greeting your mother and father and then going into another room; you were to be seen and not heard unless spoken to. Our parent-child relationship never went too far past the roles of provider and beneficiary and neither did our conversations, but I could tell he was a very reserved man. I'm also told he was very smart (to acquire such wealth I assumed he would be). He was the kind of person who, if surrounded by five different people telling him completely different stories, would listen closely to each of them as they spoke and make them feel like they were fully heard and completely right. Incidentally, before I was born, my father had been a diplomat. It was clear by the way he would walk into any room and command respect. He was the only one in his family who became successful, and he provided for them all – siblings, cousins, uncles, aunts, whoever – giving them whatever they asked for or needed. My father was the generous, loyal, and stable foundation on which all of our lives were built. When he was alive, I didn't fully understand the role he played, but once my father was gone, his impact was impossible to miss.

## More Than Just A Girl

His death was sudden. One day, my dad told the family he wasn't feeling well and immediately went to the hospital. Doctors say he was gone the moment he arrived. That same day my older half-sister, my mom's daughter from a previous marriage, came to pick up my sister and I from school. Unannounced, unexpected, and telling us nothing, she called my sister and I to take us home. While our older half-sister rode with us on the minibus, my other sister was crying the whole way. She'd always been, in my opinion, too sensitive. At that point, in my blissfully unaware state, there was no reason to believe anything was wrong. I was a no-tears sort of person, so I had zero tolerance for her emotion. What I knew at the moment was that we did not have to finish the school day, and the non-school time was being wrecked by her crying and wailing. Annoyed, I criticized her like any other 10-year-old picking on a sibling. "You always cry over stupid things," I shouted. "You need to be quiet!" My half-sister stayed silent. I think back to those minutes on the ride when my worst problem in life was my sister crying.

When we got home, our family told us right then that our dad had died. My sister, who had instinctively known that something was very wrong the moment our school day came to a surprising end, broke down completely distraught and almost inconsolable. She didn't know for sure before they told us, but she's always been one to pick up on the signs when something's wrong. Everyone around me was distraught, hysterical, and sobbing, but I felt a strange disconnection from it all. It was weird to me, especially because my dad had just visited us at school maybe a week or so before that. The memory of how he looked and smelled was still too real, and how I felt in his presence was still so palpable. And even though I could see how upset everyone was around me, I noticed how I wasn't really that sad. It could have been because I was much younger, but my sister and I were only about a year apart, and she was bawling. Then I thought maybe it was because I barely saw my dad while he was alive. He never lived with us. He'd come once a week to visit for like an hour or two, and maybe once every six months, he'd spend the night. I felt no sense of loss. Even at his funeral, as everyone cried their eyes out, all I could do was look down at my dress. I was old enough to be aware of what was going on, but wrestled with the reality. It was like I was waiting to be awoken from a horrible dream.

Regardless of where you live or your culture, when someone with great wealth dies, the people who surrounded the deceased during their life all behave in the same way. They grab at what they can get. Greed turns otherwise good and loving people into horrible creatures who will stop at nothing to get what they believe to be their fair share. And if there are many, many people who were depending on the deceased for their well-being, it makes matters worse. Greed mixed with desperation breeds cruelty.

My father's wealth was vast. He owned houses, property, land, equipment, companies, and other valuable assets. He used it all to support five families as well as friends and extended family members. At the time of his death, my dad didn't have a will. Or if he did have one, it somehow disappeared in the days following his death. What should have happened under Ugandan law was the appointment of an executor. What actually happened was a few of my father's family members appointing themselves as executors to commence stealing everything. Six months later, they all gathered together for a meeting. By then, basically everything my dad had built was disappearing. Everyone was stealing what they could off his farm which housed cattle, corn, sugar cane, and machinery. My father owned many properties, but the house that my mother, sister, and I lived in was in a prime location, making it one of the more valuable and desirable assets of his. Connected to that through my mother was the hotel he owned which she managed for him.

It wasn't as common for women in Uganda to be business managers at that time, and it was even less common to find highly successful ones. My mother was a formidable exception. The hotel she ran was very profitable, mostly because of her intelligence and strong business prowess. But all my father's family saw was the profit. As family members became greedier, our home and the hotel my mother managed were at the top of the list of assets up for grabs. They became more desperate to sell things off to maintain their dependent lifestyles. This must have been why, when we arrived for the large family meeting, their first order of business was to fire my mother as manager of the hotel. My mom had already been through so much and now I was watching as some of my aunties, uncles, and step-brothers were saying that she could no longer work.

In Africa, there are very few high-paying jobs. Even fewer options if you are a woman. And when my father died, my mother became a single woman with two children. Her job at the hotel meant that for nearly half a year since he'd been gone, she was able to continue sending us to school, feeding us, clothing us, and keeping us in a comparatively charming home in a good part of town. Now we were sitting in a room filled with people who used to be my family, and they were taking away our means for living. I remember looking around at the people in the room. Women who had been loving and kind throughout my childhood. Those who I had called auntie looked at my mother, sister, and me in silence, with hate spilling from their eyes. The men who I'd always called uncle and brother spoke to my mother so dismissively and with such finality. None would condescend to meet her eye or give her a reason. I was furious.

Throughout the scene that was unfolding, I had been sitting quietly, dutifully, and respectfully. Everything in my upbringing had taught my body to sit silently while the adults were speaking. But my mind was in full revolt. I felt a burning in my chest that grew hotter and hotter, rising and spreading until my whole body felt like it was vibrating, almost like a simmering pot of water just before it breaks into a boil. One word was screaming inside my head: "No!" My mother looked like she was crumbling, shrinking into herself, and already dissolving into the despair of uncertainty that was to come. I felt afraid and confused. This made no sense. It must be a mistake. I looked at one of the women, and the words tore out of my small body, "Auntie, it sounds like you're telling my mom that she cannot get money from the hotel anymore, but I am going to school, and I need money for that." I couldn't stay silent even if I was supposed to. I just felt like maybe they forgot that my mom had two daughters to take care of and that we all relied on her job at the hotel. But once I finished, my auntie just screamed at me.

"Don't even go there! I am *not* your aunt, and whatever you want to do, you will have to figure out with your mom." She said. Snapped back into my place, I made my way out of the room. As I was leaving, I heard her berating and belittling my mother for my bad behavior. Once I was gone, my mom tells me they accused her of being a bad parent, telling her she obviously didn't discipline her daughters correctly. One of them had just spoken out in the middle of an adult meeting, and that type of behavior, which was a direct reflection on her, was unforgivable. They told my mom we were going to have to move out of our house. We had exactly one week to stay in the house's storage room before we had to be gone altogether. In a final act of cruelty, my father's family disconnected the electricity to the room, guaranteeing that we'd move out in the time given.

My mom cried so much I couldn't even believe she had tears left. Her eyes seemed like they were permanently red and puffy. Her smile had all but vanished entirely from her face. She became ghost-like, totally removed from the land of the living. It was clear she was struggling to cope, but at that time, it was understandable. She'd just lost a great husband and father to her children, and now we were staying in one of the storage rooms on our property, stuffed inside like sardines in a can compared to how we lived before. Things were happening so fast I couldn't register exactly what they meant or recognize where my life was headed. The extended family that was harmonious and cooperative before my father's death was fragmenting as people began to see one another as a threat to their own existence. No one knew what that existence would look like in the absence of my father. I realized how many new faces I'd seen – family members I had never met before and neighbors who I'd maybe seen in passing but never knew the true place that my dad held in their lives. There were constantly people coming around saying things like, "Who will pay my son's tuition? I can't afford my rent for this month without his help. What are we going to do without him?" I wondered what life would look like for all of us moving forward.

After that whole situation, we stopped talking to the extended family for about a year and a half. We would have gone on quite happily, never thinking of them or speaking to them, had it not been for the expectation that we participate in the *last funeral rites*. In my culture, when the head of the family dies, everyone gathers two years later, the will is read, and a new family head is named and introduced. Even though my father had no will, and everything in his estate was stolen, sold, or spent, it was still necessary for everyone to gather back together for the rites. Typically, the last funeral rites is a huge ceremony where 200 people or more are likely to attend. The more respected the person was in life, the more people generally gathered. My father was an important man, so his last funeral rites gathering was sizable and spanned several days. And because of the in-fighting, drama, and turmoil that we had all suffered in the two years since his death, it was especially dramatic. Adding to the drama were my aunts and uncles, who were all there, along with my step-brothers. Initially, this was the core group of family members who had teamed up and betrayed us. Now, I saw that my step-siblings were distancing themselves because they had, in turn, been betrayed by my father's family, specifically his brothers and sisters, who had stolen everything from them. Then there was my mom's group of friends and her family that still supported us. By then, everything that my dad had accumulated in his lifetime was pretty much all gone. We knew that there would be nothing for us, but it would have been extremely disrespectful not to attend. Hoping to avoid further conflict, we physically distanced ourselves as best we could. It also helped remembering how the people who had ruined us had gone on to ruin one another.

You see, after our former extended family demanded we move out, they attempted to sell our old house and split the money. What they didn't know was there is only one person who could actually sell it – my dad's one legal wife. In Uganda, a woman is considered a man's wife if the two share children and live together in a traditional way. My mother, as well as the majority of the others, were this type of wife. The legal wife is the one recognized by the church, and for my father, it was either the second or third woman he took as a wife and had an actual wedding with. Only because she was the one that my father took to church and married in a ceremony, she was the legal wife. As his legal wife, this woman was the only person who could actually sell the house and make any kind of profit. The day after we moved out, the new owner began demolishing it. At 5 a.m., I walked past it on my way to school and ran back home as soon as I saw it to tell my mom and my sister. It instantly became a celebratory moment for us. It was the one and only time I saw my mother light up during that dreadful experience. We just laughed at how funny it was that the family members rushed to kick us out of the house only for none of them to even get to keep it or its profits. It served them right. My mom had been left with no job, no place to live and two growing daughters to feed, and they never seemed to care. For one fleeting moment, we felt a shred of triumph. But a year and a half later, that same aunt who I'd talked back to at the meeting that decided our new reality saw fit to continue to kick us while we were trying to pick ourselves up from the ground.

We'd successfully avoided interacting with our former extended family members for the majority of the weekend. That is, until the end, when the family and other attendees came together in a group for the final portion of the gathering. There, in front of everyone, the intimidation, bullying, and threats against my mother rekindled. The same auntie who confronted her at the family meeting attacked again. "You gave birth to worthless girls," she said, speaking in our native Lugandan tongue. Almost spitting through her teeth, she continued, "They are nothing, and they will move about the world aimlessly." As harsh as that sounds, that's not even the direct translation of what she really meant. In our culture, that comment is a curse. You also can't hear the abusive, condescending tone that still rings out in my mind to this day. The shame and anger I felt at hearing it still cuts like a knife when I conjure up the memory. I couldn't believe that this woman whom I'd barely met and only interacted with once before would say such a thing about us. Even at that age, I understood how important it was to have a son. I understood having a male heir meant someone who could run things after the father was gone, someone who could work and take care of the family while carrying its name into history. According to our beliefs and traditions, only a man could assume that role once it was vacant. I instinctively knew that being a boy was a good thing. I knew that my sister and I weren't treated the same as our brothers, but we'd always been treated with respect until that moment. I'd also never witnessed my mother being treated with disrespect, disregard, or disdain because the children she'd given birth to just so happened to be female. Now, this aunt felt it fitting to curse us so viciously. With that one exchange, she was predicting, even hoping in the most damning way possible, that we would live in ghettos for the rest of our lives. And that either we were going to have a bunch of kids by different men or we would become prostitutes. The other family members' faces made it clear that her words were the consensus of the group. Because my sister and I were 'just girls,' in their eyes we would never amount to anything. They weren't willing to share the last of my dad's estate because they wholeheartedly believed we would waste it. Now that he wasn't around to advocate for us, apparently we were no longer worthy of the chance his wealth could give for us to grow up in a good family, go to good schools, get degrees, and good jobs.

I count that small stretch of minutes as the single most defining moment of my life because it was exactly then that everything changed for me. I had to prove my family wrong and make my mom proud that she'd had daughters, so I promised myself that I would do whatever I had to do to make that happen. I was going to make something of myself because I knew I deserved more. Standing next to my mother and sister that day, with all of the belongings we bought packed and ready to go, I knew with the end of my father's final funeral rites behind us, we would never need to see these horrible people again. They had tried to break us, but we were still there – asking for nothing, taking nothing, needing nothing. Not from them. Our previous family members had not been able to destroy us, as they ruined themselves. The words of my auntie's curse still rung in my ears as I raised my chin and smiled with every ounce of strength and pride I felt brimming from within. I waved enthusiastically, shouting as loud as I could so that everyone could hear the child addressing the adult who had not given her leave to speak, "Ok, bye auntie! The worthless girls are leaving now." From that moment on, my life purpose was to find a way to succeed despite everything stacked against me. I was sure I was not a worthless girl, so I would make them see.

## Taking Control

Unfortunately, no matter how nasty my aunt came across, there was some truth behind what she was saying. I was a young girl who would grow up without proper support in a developing society predominantly run by men. I couldn't help who my father was, what he had, or how we'd all gotten into this predicament either. They were saying my dad had been poisoned by the woman he'd been trying to make his wife. He'd owned a farm, and she was living there and managing it for not very long, maybe a few months, but she wanted the property to herself. My family says that woman killed my dad so she'd have it all, which inevitably left me and so many others with absolutely nothing. What could I have truly done about any of this? I couldn't ever bring my dad back to life. I didn't have a time machine to go to the past and tell him not to marry that woman or change our traditions to be more accepting of who I was and less accepting of his lifestyle. And there was no wand to wave that could magically turn me or my sister into a boy so we'd have a chance to stay on the property and let our mom keep her job. Entirely without my consent, I'd been thrust out of my comfort zone by the acts of others. There were so many things that had brought me to such an unpredictable place, but the moment I vowed to never become the woman my aunt said I'd turn out to be was the exact moment I took back the reins. Once I'd given my life a new purpose and a strong reason to fulfill it, I'd found my 'why' and I finally had a sense of control over how things would go moving forward. And I haven't loosened my death grip on those reins since.

Most people like to use the words 'purpose' and 'why' interchangeably, but to me they're two separate things. The way I look at it is, if your purpose is the end result, then your why makes up the means to get there. It's like an ingredient to the ultimate recipe:

## WHY + PASSION = PURPOSE

The truth is, everyone has a purpose. It's essentially the road map that shows all of the decisions and actions we've taken throughout our lives. And if passion is the vehicle that takes us to meet our purpose, then our why is the gas. It's what gets us out of bed every morning and makes us do the things we do every day to pursue this purpose. I've noticed that having this deeper understanding of my purpose is the single greatest reason why I've been able to accomplish everything I have at this point in my life. Every decision I've made and step I've taken has been directed – meant to go toward the life I wanted instead of the one other people told me I was meant to have. And anytime I was unsure of whether I was doing the right things or if I was feeling tired, I remembered my why, and it kept me going because I had something to prove. In those moments, I'd hear the words of my aunt, and the strength of my resolve would come rushing back.

I've often wondered if I would have accomplished as much as I have if that moment with my aunt never occurred. I have always landed at the same conclusion. No…I wouldn't. None of us absolutely need to know our 'why' to fulfill our life's purpose. There are plenty of people who live their lives without ever putting any meaning behind their actions. However, those aren't usually the people we admire or look up to. We tend to look up to those who do things differently, separate themselves from the crowd, and follow the beat of their own drum. People who put meaning behind their actions and who show the world why they are doing what they do have direction, focus, and ambition to go well beyond the point where others would stop. If you never have a sense of where you're going or why you're moving, then you run the risk of focusing on the things you 'should' be doing instead of those things aligned with your true and unique purpose. For those of us who know why we live our lives the way we do, to outsiders it always seems like we have it all figured out. But that's not true for anyone. We just have a clearer vision of all of our steps, making it easier for us to take them.

When I was 12 years old, I unexpectedly took the first step toward fulfilling my purpose because I had something that was pushing me toward it. I discovered my why, and that directed my steps, making me absolutely sure I wouldn't wander through life aimlessly. If you are luckier than me, you will not have to encounter a series of dreadful life experiences to spark a well of ambition and drive that help you fulfill your life's purpose. You can look at any goal you hope to accomplish in your business, career, or even your relationships and personal life as your purpose – some end result that you're working toward. Having a why gives your pursuit toward that goal meaning, and in turn, you'll be much more motivated to achieve it. For me, a painful situation revealed my why and that's true for many people. Anger, shame, and pain were the catalyst, but it's not the only way for you to realize your motivation. Your experience does not need to be the same to create that exact defining moment in your own life. Just think about what it is that drives you. What is something that touches you so powerfully that when you think of it, you feel energized, driven, and ambitious? Maybe it's some grave injustice in the world you've promised yourself you must change. Or maybe it's the smile on your child's face when they're their happiest. It could even be the gratifying feeling you get when you finally fit into those old jeans. What is something that you would sacrifice your time, money, sleep, or certain relationships or activities for? Is there a belief you have or a cause you care about? When you think about them, does it make you feel courageous enough to take the risks needed to see them through? Whatever it is, once you find the reason for achieving your goals, you'll become laser-focused on them and nearly unstoppable. Because once you find your why, you immediately take command of what happens in your life, and you'll feel the switch from surviving to thriving. The girl I was when I walked away from the final exchange that left me cast aside and written out of my dad's estate was a completely different person from the one who walked into it. I had a new trajectory for my life and the drive to get me there. I didn't know how I would make it, but I knew I'd figure it out.

## The Secret Ingredient

Thinking back to when our week in the storage room was up and we were no longer allowed to live on the property my dad had owned, I realize this is when I truly began my journey toward transformation. Thankfully, we were never utterly homeless. My mom had a house she owned herself, so we packed what was left of our things and moved there immediately. We had no car or truck, so we picked up and carried things from the old house to the new, making multiple trips back and forth. The family told us we could not take much of the furniture or things my father provided to us, so there was little to move.

Nothing like the house I grew up in, our new home was small and felt almost as cramped as the storage room. There wasn't much space outside to play, and there was barely any space indoors to live. Red dust from the dirt in the streets clung to our clothes and shoes as we made our way onto the identically dusted floors in our new space. One moment I was running across our lush estate with my sister. We were playing as children do before going off to school. We'd have full bellies of breakfast made of tea with sugar, fresh milk and fruits, hot porridge and savory meats. Now we were leaving our immense acreage for a one-room, tin-roofed shack in the slums, jammed tightly between many others. And I didn't know when my next meal would come. I looked into the empty area where cooking and eating were to happen. I was unaware at that point that there would be an uncountable number of nights ahead when I would stand there, body empty and aching with hunger. Almost daily, the electricity would go out. When it rained, the entire street would flood for hours. In Kampala, it rains very often, so each time it did, our home would be filled with rust-colored water that could reach as high as our waists, forcing us to stand or sit upright through the night until it receded. The runoff from the unpaved, busy city streets mixed with the under-developed sanitation system filled our home with diseased water. My sister and I were constantly sick.

I so desperately wanted to go back to my old life so that I could appreciate it more. Only now, with the safety and stability of that life gone, did I understand how lucky I'd been. But as the days passed, I noticed there were many others worse off than us. I observed how easy it was for people to become completely homeless. Everyone in our new neighborhood was struggling, and many didn't make enough money to pay their rent. It wasn't uncommon for a family to come home, kids from school or parents from work, and find their front door chained closed with a large lock to keep them from getting in or taking their things out. That was another thing I knew I could be thankful for. I was glad that we at least had a place to live. We had absolutely nothing else besides this home my mom owned, but it was more than what most people around us had. When I would see those locks, it would instantly remind me that things could be far worse than they already were. As terrible as it was, my mother owned our home. And there was no landlord, greedy family member, or domineering man who could take it from us. If we didn't own our home, it might've just been a matter of time before we were locked out too. For that, I was grateful.

People treated us as if we were better off just because we didn't have a landlord to answer to, and that helped me look at our situation in a totally different light. Noticing how I wasn't the only one who realized how lucky we were made me appreciate my present situation more for what it was. I realized that no matter what negative situation you find yourself in, you can always find something positive within that situation to focus on. And I learned later in life that gratitude is the great multiplier. The more good things you look for in a situation, the more good things that show up for you to find. It's almost like magic. Look for the positive. The moment you find it, you find a reason to be grateful. And then you'll find another, and another, until eventually your perception of your situation is permanently changed. Our gratitude is what keeps us grounded. It launches us out of the past, where things are out of our control, and into the present, where we have opportunities to take action for the better. It's simply taking notice of your circumstances and surroundings and finding the good in them. When I left my dad's property, I had no idea what my next step would be, but each time I became grateful for something, it reminded me of my why and my purpose. I've successfully used this technique in business when I've encountered barriers and dead ends.

Gratitude costs nothing, but it's definitely worth more than all of the riches in the world. However, when you give thanks, you have to mean it for the magic to work, and it takes practice to truly *feel* thankful for anything. Saying 'thank you' is great, and it's a fantastic start, but it's not enough. Having my why gave everything I did meaning, and it was exactly what made it much easier to feel grateful. Learning gratitude was monumental for me. In those first few months in the slums, I learned to take nothing for granted. Whatever I could find in my environment that made me happy, the reason behind that happiness usually had something to do with my new reason for living. Whenever I saw a lock on a door, I remembered the home that my dad's family couldn't take away from us. That would lead me to think about why that home was so important to me. Having a place to live meant that I had somewhere to sleep. Having a place to sleep meant safety and security. When I realized I was safe, and my house was secure, I could focus on what I had in my power to improve our situation. Learning gratitude kept me focused on the present and rooted in reality. My focus shifted to what I had rather than what I lost. The skill to train my focus in this way has been an invaluable tool on my journey to success.

Having gratitude isn't a requirement for reaching success, but it does make the road much easier to navigate. For me, it became my secret ingredient in the recipe for my new purpose. Gratitude is exactly what made me into the resourceful woman and entrepreneur I am today. It's because of gratitude that I can look at anything and see what I can use at my disposal instead of focusing on what I'm missing. Without gratitude, I would have been constantly thinking about how my life used to be before my dad died and what things I could do if he was still around. I might have obsessed over the memory of him giving me extra money for snacks instead of figuring out how to get the money I needed for my next meal. My 10-year-old self needed time to adjust, learn, and settle into the new realization of the power of gratitude and appreciation. But slowly but surely, I learned not to dwell on the things I couldn't easily change. Recognizing the good in any situation has made it easier for me to learn from my mistakes and move on much faster from them. The feeling of gratitude is such a strong emotion that it became nearly impossible for me to feel sorry for myself or sad about what I was dealing with. That kept me optimistic, and I continued making progress toward my goals no matter how steep they were, or mysterious they seemed.

One definite way to become better at practicing gratitude is by making it a point to notice one new thing you can be grateful for each day. Maybe today it is your family, and the next it's your job, and the day after that it's for chocolate ice cream. Before you know it, you'll be at the end of the year with close to 400 completely unique things you can be grateful for. As it pertains to our goals, the things we are grateful for are what inch us closer to accomplishing the things we hope for the most. The more I recognized what I could be grateful for in my environment, the faster it was for me to find my first hustle that could change my life and upgrade my situation.

# CHAPTER 2

# Hungry For More

### A lesson on visualization

Looking back, I feel like it was my mother's painful response to my father's death that truly transformed my life. It was tremendously difficult for her to get back on her feet after his passing. To say she was sad, distraught, or even depressed in the months that followed can't begin to describe it. Any of those things would have been a step up from the place that she descended to. Often it seemed like she was just so far away from us. She became a shell of herself, moving through each day without seeming to hear, see, or engage. She was no longer present, and she didn't seem to recognize my sister and I were still there, scared, hungry, and reeling from the abrupt change to a world we didn't know or understand.

For a while, my mother stopped eating regularly, so my sister and I would go days at a time without food. Once she scraped together 5¢ and bought a glass of milk and sat alone drinking it with a far off look on her face. My sister and I hung by her side, hoping for the moment that she would snap out of her trance and hand us the glass. But her eyes didn't lock on ours the way they used to. Now it was like she saw right through us. It's actually funny to me that I don't drink milk now because of this point in my life. To this day, I can barely tolerate the taste or smell. I can only guess that I never had the chance to build up a preference for it into adulthood. Or maybe seeing my mom show how little she cared about feeding us put a permanent sour taste in my mouth.

The transformation I witnessed in my mother was so confusing. I knew her to be strong, self-assured, and assertive. She was not a woman that most people, my sister and I included, were willing to test. Before, to me, she'd been a fighter. Now she was a stranger, an imposter in my mother's body. Our half-siblings would tell us how things used to be when they were growing up before she met our dad. They'd talk about how hard our mom worked to make sure everything they needed was provided for and how this was not the woman they knew then. They described her devotion. How she'd make it a point to get them chicken or some kind of meat every weekend to eat. She'd keep them clean, neat, and dressed nicely, they went to church every week, and she always remained dedicated and attentive. Time and time again, she would put their needs above her own. This woman was no longer that person. Perhaps it shouldn't have been a surprise to any of us. We'd known that our mother's entire life had been a battle of survival, and even someone as strong as she was could eventually break.

## Moving On

My mother was born into a poor farming family in 1950. At that time in Uganda, the birth of a daughter wasn't something to celebrate. Back then, if you were a girl, you'd stay home and forgo schooling to work at home, providing whatever domestic service the family required. A daughter was not as valuable as a son, and most families simply put them to work until they were old enough to marry off to another man's family. They say my mother's father was fiercely tough and that he overworked his wife and kids mercilessly, often beating them if things weren't up to his high standards. To my grandfather, my mother and her siblings were not children. They were more like farm equipment for him to use rather than people to raise and love. They'd work over 12 hours a day starting as early as 4 am, working the land, fetching the water, planting, picking, weeding, cooking the meals, and doing whatever else needed to be done for both the family and the property. But even though they kept his farm alive, my grandfather never valued the girls he had, always seeing them as a worthless burden. So when he married my mother off at 15 years old, she saw it as a rescue. With no money, no job, no education, and no connections, marriage truly was her only chance to escape from a cruel and abusive life. Sadly, she'd find there was no bright and happy existence on the other side. Instead, her marriage was an exchange - one brutal experience for another.

My mother found her new husband to be a drunk, unopposed to working her harder than her father had, making her farm the land the entire season from dusk to dawn, often using the money from the harvest to buy more liquor. He demanded that she work far harder than she ever had and would fly into drunken rages beating her nearly to death if she didn't meet his strict demands. Somehow in that first year, in the midst of the exhaustive physical labor and the severe and frequent beatings, my mother gave birth to a son. But instead of pushing him to support his family, their son's birth only made him more demanding, abusive, and violent. To this day, my mother still has this huge scar in the middle of her skull - evidence of where this man's machete landed on her head, almost splitting it wide open when she didn't have his dinner ready on time. She was only 16 years old with no loved ones nearby or any way to provide for herself, but she knew that even her time with her son would be short-lived if she stayed to care for him. Because the next time her husband cleaved her head open with a machete, she knew she would not survive. Fighting her instincts as a mother, she chose to live and made a plan to leave.

    Sneaking out late one night and pretending to use the bathroom (since there was no indoor plumbing), my mother left the baby inside with her husband and hid in a mango tree not too far from where their house stood. Sitting high enough to remain hidden and still see the house, she waited and watched for nearly an hour as her husband angrily searched for her to soothe their crying son. Sometimes I picture my mother in that tree. A young girl. A child. The machete wound on her head still fresh. The years would have a chance to smooth it, her hair would eventually grow over it and bury it deep, but it would have still been red, angry, and puckered on that night. I see her with her eyes closed and teeth clenched, hearing her child scream and forcing back her own desire to cry. I see her gripping her hands on the branch of the mango tree, willing them to hold and begging her trembling body to stay absolutely still as her husband looked for her. But after getting no answer to his calls, he took their son over to his mother's house, went back home, turned off his kerosene lamp, and supposedly went to bed. As soon as my mother saw the lamp go out through the window, she knew it was her chance to make an escape. Quietly climbing down from the tree, she ran, going as fast and as far as she could until daybreak. When she'd made it three cities over, she finally stopped. Exhausted, dirty, and possessing nothing but the clothing she was wearing when she left her husband's house, my mother looked and looked until she found someone willing to hire her. Weeks later, she found someone trustworthy to deliver a letter to her mother, who lived on the other side of the country, letting her know she was alive and safe. After a few months of working and living alone, it was safe for my grandmother to come to my mother and help her get a job working as a maid.

Against the odds, my mother had managed to survive her first husband and began doing quite well for herself. Working and earning a good living, she started to live a whole new life. At that time, she met someone new and at first, everything went well. But after she'd stopped working to take care of their home and family, he began to change. Her new husband wasn't violent. For that, my mother was grateful. Unfortunately, he'd shown he had no ambition, was also a drunk, and terribly irresponsible, leaving his family for extended periods with no money or food. They'd had six or seven kids by then, yet he made no effort to care for the family, and there was nothing my mother could do or say to change things. Again, with nothing more than her strength, resolve, and determination my mother decided, if things were going to get better, it would be up to her to make it happen.

Soon she got a job working at a pharmacy. With her making good money, she could finally afford food and whatever else she and her children needed. Their lives began to slowly improve. Eventually, she bought her own land, built a house on it and moved the family in. But her husband never wanted to buy it. In fact, he never really wanted to do anything productive at all. Not long after my mom got her job, he'd started drinking more, dating other women, and stealing money right out of my mom's purse. She'd actually found out that he was plotting to kill her, figuring that with her gone, he could still keep the house and the land and bring in another woman to take care of it all. And for the second time, she was left without many options. Going to the police would not help. Protections against domestic abuse as we know them did not exist in Uganda, and plotting to kill someone was not something that would attract police attention. If my mother's husband wanted her gone, he could make that happen. She was helpless. Once more, she had to choose - stay and be killed, or leave and live. Again, she chose to live. Not long after, she met and married my father. And with him, she found the first and only man who was good to her, cared for her, and was dedicated to his family.

It would take me years to understand my mother's history and how it resulted in the person I was seeing during the months we were first destitute. She'd done so much in her life and had beat the odds so many times before, but now, it was like I was looking at a completely different person. This determined woman ran through the night to freedom but no longer had the strength to get up and feed her hungry children. Despite the fact she wore the same scar in the middle of her head from when she narrowly escaped death at the hands of the man who was supposed to love her, the woman in front of me was miles away from the woman who'd stayed in the mango tree all those years ago. I never wondered if she loved my sister and me, but it got to a point where she wasn't the caring mother she'd been before. It was clear that my dad's death had drastically changed my mom, and it suddenly became frighteningly clear-cut to me - I could no longer rely on her to keep me alive. She was lost to grief, and there was no one for my sister and I to turn to. Our former extended family had utterly abandoned us. It was so bad that on any given day, one of them could see us out on the street and they'd either ignore us entirely or treat us as if we were trash on the side of the road. We were suffering, and it seemed that nobody in the world cared. I was the youngest of all of my mother's children, but that didn't matter. I was only 10 years old, but I knew I couldn't keep waiting for other people to change my life. No one ever stepped in to help take care of us, so I felt like it was all up to me to step up and get to work.

    I came to understand the more money I made, the less hungry I was. If I had to learn a million new things, then I was ready. If I had to spend entire days thinking about ways to find food, then I was more than willing. Even if I had to stand outside for hours in flooding rains selling whatever I could find, then I was going to do it. Every bit of success was a direct result of my effort. I knew I couldn't keep waiting for other people to change my life for me. And when I stopped worrying about what all those older people *should* have been doing to help, it became easier for me to focus on what I could be doing independently. I was the only person in my life that I could fully trust to consistently comfort, feed, clothe, and keep me safe. There was absolutely no chance that I'd let myself wither away because I was too sad, young, or lazy to get up and prevent it from happening. I had so few options, but I was determined to find a way. Whatever it took, I was going to have more for myself.

Thankfully, I'd already started selling popcorn to our neighbors before moving out of the storage room on our old property. A few months before my dad died, we'd gone somewhere and had popcorn someone had been selling. I thought it was so cool that this person had a popcorn machine and how amazing it was that people paid them for it. Something in my little mind clicked then and I understood. The popcorn on its own was nice, but what made it especially good was the fact that other people wanted it and would give you something even more valuable to get it. I decided that I wanted to sell it too. I remember I wanted to make money to help my friends with their school tuition. They lived near us, but they weren't as well off and their father was in prison. In Uganda, school is not free as it is in other places. To go to any school, you have to pay. Basic day schools could cost up to $40 a semester, and better boarding schools could go up to a few hundred dollars for the same amount of time. If I could sell popcorn, then I'd be able to make some money to help my friends out who were struggling to attend. There also wasn't anyone around our house that sold popcorn at the time. I understood, without knowing it, that without any competition, I would do very well. And I did.

The first time I sold popcorn, I made a lot of money. Running my machine on the side of the house, the smells circulating throughout our neighborhood, people came in crowds to buy bags at 5¢ apiece. I'd sell out in a matter of hours. The neighbors began looking forward to holidays because I would be home from boarding school and my popcorn stand would be open for business. It got so popular that once the neighbors discovered we were making good money, they also started selling it. All these adults were copying my idea. I loved the feeling of validation that came with the success of my first business, but it also taught me about competition. I had created a brand, and being the first, it kept a lot of my customers still coming to me.

Because I had been successful with my popcorn business before our move, it was easy to start back up in our new home. Our profits were good, but it was hardly enough to take care of any of us the way we were used to. I kept thinking to myself how I would just get a job if people would let me, but I was 10. It was obvious no one in their right mind was going to hire me for anything lucrative, or even legal. I assumed I would get a good job once I was old enough, but until then, I did what I could and kept my mind open and eyes peeled. I trusted that I would eventually find more opportunities to turn my efforts into cash.

## Whatever It Takes

Every day after school, I'd go out to sell popcorn to the people returning home from work. We chose popcorn to sell because most people liked to eat it either as an evening snack or in the morning as a quick breakfast with tea. I would be in school from about 8 a.m. to 5 p.m., so after school was the perfect time to catch my customers on their commutes. If I didn't have school, like on the weekend or during a school term holiday, I'd sell in the morning from 8 a.m. until about 11 am, and then again in the evenings from about 5 p.m. or 6 p.m. until 8 p.m. or 9 p.m.. Business was great since popcorn was so popular. It was also an easy thing for me to bag and sell since the corn was inexpensive and not too heavy for my customers or me to carry around. I was pleased with what I'd been able to accomplish at that point, but there was a limit to my time and the amount of money I could make from my efforts. I needed something more.

Then one day right out of the blue, one of my customers gave me my next business idea. I don't remember exactly how it went. Either they said something like, "Oh man, the electricity is going to be out again tonight. I wish you were selling candles too." He may have offered me money to get him candles, or I offered to buy him some. Whatever it was, I knew that if I did start selling candles alongside the popcorn, I'd at least have one guaranteed customer. That one was enough for me. Plus, I agreed with them. Candles were such a great idea that I couldn't believe I hadn't thought of it myself. It was just so obvious. The electricity in our neighborhood went out almost daily, so people needed candles. But for as much as they were needed, people didn't always have them on hand. You'd have to get them when you realized you needed them, or remember to buy them when the supply was low. I was already walking around selling my popcorn, I figured candles were light and easy enough to carry along. So with my popcorn profits, I bought supplies to make the candles and started selling them too. That way, people could buy them both at the same time to have in the evenings. It became a very easy sell because people would come to buy popcorn, see the candles, and realize that they should also be buying them for later when their electricity went out. Or, they would remember that I sold candles, and while purchasing those, see the popcorn, and think about how nice it would be as an evening snack. And since the electricity went out almost every day, I was quickly making more money. Though I didn't know it at the time, I was learning another basic concept of entrepreneurship: look for something that people need and find an easier, better, or cheaper way to give it to them. I was now making even more money with the same amount of time, but it still wasn't enough. I knew I was working for way more than just my next meal, so I'd have to do way more to get there.

Between school and my popcorn and candle business, I had very little spare time. But I was still focused on pursuing more opportunities for making money. On weekends and holidays, I'd have between 12 p.m. and 5 p.m. when there wasn't anyone really around for me to sell my regular items to. This became the perfect time for my next business venture. My neighborhood was more or less a ghetto, but the surrounding area was rapidly developing and becoming more industrial. This meant there was plenty of scrap metal near my house with several people very interested in buying. The same business operators nearby were way too busy to gather it themselves. So I started spending my free time gathering the scraps and selling them to the hardware stores and garages in my neighborhood. Though it was hard work, it was lucrative. It was a way of using the few hours I had available to make even more money. At that point, my little brain was conditioned to work like an entrepreneur, and I began automatically looking around for opportunities I could turn into new business endeavors. What did I have around me that was valuable to someone else, and how could I use that to make money for myself? I noticed things, kept lists of ideas in my head, and waited for the time when the pieces fell together.

After doing all of this for a little while, I noticed a cooking show playing on my neighbor's TV one afternoon. We didn't have our own, so I'd watch theirs through their window. On the show, they shared a recipe for a cake that I thought looked delicious. The ingredients were easy to find and not very expensive, and the technique was not too complicated. I wrote down the recipe and began to think. My current customer base consisted of people on the go. I imagined many of them could use something more substantial to eat than popcorn. Using the profits from my candle sales, I invested in the ingredients. Pretty soon, I was making and selling individual cakes people could easily buy from me to eat on-the-go. Adding that hustle brought me to four streams of income total, but I didn't stop there. Doing these things helped me learn the basics of entrepreneurship that have been the foundation of my success, but it wasn't the lifestyle I ultimately wanted. I knew what I used to have, so I knew what was possible beyond that. And as much as I enjoyed making money, I liked having the things I needed without having to spend that money even more.

The Kabaka's Palace, the home of Buganda's[1] king, was close enough to my home that I could occasionally go there with a group of my friends. The estate grounds are such a stark contrast to what

---

[1] Buganda is a subnational kingdom within the country of Uganda composed of the Ganda people - traditionally fifty-two clans that make up the largest ethnic group in Uganda.

I was used to seeing every day as I was growing up that I was always in awe of its existence. It taught me to aspire, and I couldn't stay away. Expansive, luxurious, clean, comfortable – it was everything that I wanted in life. The Palace at Mengo epitomizes the phrase, *the grass is always greener on the other side.* It's home to a rich stretch of vegetation and greenery that the surrounding areas haven't seen for decades. Tied to a centuries-old legacy of war and traditions of lack, it's a place that evokes many different emotions and ideas for different people. For a quick, resourceful, and brave kid like me, it meant free food during slow times. As profitable as my businesses were, there were still days where what I made just wasn't enough. If we didn't have food at home or the money to buy it, the other kids and I would climb the palace fence and pick fruits off the many trees on the property. And if there weren't too many palace guards on patrol, we actually used to take some food from inside the palace and bring it back home to help feed our families. They definitely had enough to spare, so I never really felt bad about it, but the work was easier said than done. Timing, speed, and quick thinking were essential. In Uganda, unlike in the United States, kids jumping a fence and stealing from the home of the king would not be treated as "mischief" or "kids being kids." If caught, the best we could hope for was a beating. The worst was too frightening to consider. But hunger makes a kid desperate, and desperation makes the risk seem worth it. Besides, they weren't going to miss the food we took, and they definitely didn't need it as badly as we did. If anything, it was all kind of fun and exciting for me to be doing those things. Sometimes, it would feel like an adventure or this fantastic journey where I got to leave the cares of my childhood behind because I had many. I would feel liberated and empowered. With practice, my band of royal thieves and I got quite good at making it over the palace fence and we took our chances often.

Despite the fact I was part of an occasional royal-stealing kid gang, I like to think of myself as a good kid during this time in my life. I was the youngest of the family and the only one doing everything in my power to help. That should have been something that mattered to the adults in the world. Something that they would see as an admirable quality. But this was Uganda. And children in Uganda were meant to be obedient and respectful, not ambitious and admirable. I remember people whispering in my mother's ear, questioning her fitness as a parent and judging her for letting her young daughter stay out so late selling things. If you let my mom tell these stories herself of everything I did to help us eat on those days when she didn't seem to care that much, she would say I was rebellious. She disapproved of me staying out late, or spending all of my time selling goods in the streets or daydreaming of ways to get out of Uganda. We would argue sometimes, but I never stopped doing what I was doing. I couldn't stop. Even if it was challenging, it was clear that no adult would be picking up the slack if I obeyed my elders' wishes. In fact, with several different side hustles came several other obstacles I had to constantly navigate.

Witch doctors in Uganda were continually looking for kids to abduct and sacrifice. Families would pay them to help heal their illnesses, gain wealth, or accomplish anything the witch doctors would tell them they could do to get their money. Children would disappear suddenly and often, and later their bodies would be found without their heads, thoughtlessly discarded like garbage on the outskirts of their communities. It was said that the witch doctors would do spiritual rituals on the bodies, tossing them and burying the heads at the sites of new properties bought by wealthy businessmen. Other times, they'd harvest the organs and sell them on the black market, or use the remains for more rituals. I knew these stories as a child and knew, like every other mother, father, and child in my community, that it was a real and possible threat. And as scary as that all sounds, I didn't give it any of my attention. I honestly didn't think it would happen to me. Someone had told me that to be sacrificed, you had to be pure. I believed my pierced ears instantly absolved me of purity and made me safe from abduction. Plus, I had far too many things to occupy myself with other than the thought of *possibly* being sacrificed. If it happened, I couldn't control that. But what if nothing happened? That's exactly what I was banking on.

In addition to the potential of being murdered by ritual sacrifice was the possibility that I would be eternally damned for cultural sacrilege. Let me explain. In Uganda, there are, for lack of a better explanation, clans. My family and I were part of the sheep clan, which meant that we could not eat, kill, or use sheep. The wax in the candles I sold was made of sheep fat, which I didn't know until after I sunk my popcorn profits into purchasing it. All my life, I'd been told that, as a member of the sheep clan, I would break out in an allergic reaction and get a terrible lethal infection, complete with a fever, rash, and liquefying body parts if I touched sheep's meat. And here I was with several pounds of processed, former sheep parts that I not only had to melt using pans and dishes that we would subsequently eat from, but also that I would have to handle with my bare hands as I carried and sold them. I was clearly doomed. But something in me decided that the potential loss of equity from getting rid of that lump of wax would feel even worse than death. So, I took a deep breath and began. Time passed, and there was no rash, no burning skin, no eyeballs melting out of my head. I exhaled. And when customers would say, *Isn't that wax made of sheep's fat? Don't you belong to the Sheep clan? You know you can't eat any part of the sheep, or else you will break out in an allergic reaction and get a terrible infection, right? Don't even let the melted wax touch your skin or you'll be sorry...* I just smiled, thanked them, and kept going.

And stealing is not a widely accepted practice anywhere in the world, so all of my days spent sneaking around at Mengo Palace weren't always a walk in the park. We were not so lucky once, and the guards spotted us, so we ran into the dungeons created during one of the presidential wars. Having been home to generations of royalty, the palace had seen more than its fair share of bloody rebellions, especially when President Obote exiled the king. The cells of the palace prison had seen hundreds of prisoners of war and unfortunate souls who had betrayed past administrations. The evidence of all of that suffering, violence, and death was plainly there to see that first day we ran inside. The cold, dark, wet dungeons were exactly as they're typically depicted in movies and TV. The air was unavoidably thick with despair. The first few cells where the light and outside atmosphere could still find their way in were not as bad. Palace employees had cleaned them up, and though they were still shocking, they were not horrifying. But with the palace guards chasing us, we continued going deeper. The ground was wet with standing water, and we could feel the bones of the bodies underneath our feet. At some point, palace officials had run electrical wire through the prison floors to keep the prisoners in their cells. Anyone standing in that water was electrocuted when the switch was activated. We eventually made it back to the cells where no one had been for years. Choosing one as far back as we could, we ate whatever we'd been able to carry down and waited for the guards to get tired of chasing us. While waiting, we cleaned up the cell where we sat, planning ahead to have a hiding place if we were ever spotted and chased again. We would come back to this place several more times, once even trying to cook a stolen chicken, until the guards saw smoke and we had to run. I'm not sure why it didn't bother me to move skulls and other bones from the cell we were in to a neighboring one. I suppose we understood that we needed a place to hide where the adults would not want to go, but we didn't necessarily care about those things. In our minds, we weren't really stealing from these people, nor entirely in danger, no matter what our escape looked like. Staving off starvation was more important to us than avoiding slow guards and old bones.

Living near the palace definitely played a considerable role in my childhood. The tourists it attracted helped me turn decent profits selling goods nearby. The food was plentiful and protected by people who, fortunately, didn't overexert themselves trying to catch kids with sticky fingers. That palace sustained me in more ways than one, and it taught me so many things about who I was, what I was willing to do to reach my goals, and what life could look like once I did. It's a little shocking to think of how eager I was to agree to go further into those decrepit torture chambers simply because people weren't allowed down there, making them the perfect hiding places for kids like us. Why didn't I see the danger in those torture chambers? Where was my fear of being caught by the palace guards? What child would not be scared out of her mind by stories of head-chopping witch doctors, running for the safety of her home the minute the sun went down? I'd started to recognize that things never went perfectly as I found my footing as an entrepreneur, but a few challenging moments were worth more than being paralyzed in fear and not doing anything at all. I understood the danger. I just wouldn't let the fear stop me from reaching my goals. So when I'd eat the fruits of my labors with the abandoned skulls of the cave's past prisoners locked in my sights, I couldn't help but smile and feel accomplished. Everything I'd been through had led up to that one sweet moment when I could bite into that ripe mango. Fear became the least of my worries, if it was even a factor at all. I wasn't going to let fear come between me and that feeling of satisfaction, especially since it didn't pose any immediate threat to me. In those dungeons, I learned how fear wasn't a deciding factor if you're making choices and taking actions. Not if you want to succeed. That's another thing I really admire about children. They're fearless. They barely have any sense of risk or concern for their individual well-being. To most adults, blinding ourselves to the possibilities of pain is preposterous. But to a kid, worrying about the painful consequences of an action you haven't even done yet is even more mind boggling.

Not too long ago, I had to rush my son to the hospital because he fell out of the tree in our yard and broke his arm. I still can't believe he even climbed high enough to do that. He's not very big, but he didn't care. Worrying about how strong he was or how the height of his climb might have affected how far he fell was never a thing for him. My 10-year-old son was utterly determined to climb the big tree in our yard for whatever reasons his little body could muster up, so off he went. I'm happy I can say he's fine now. Just like any other kid his age who gets back on their bike after busting their knee, he's eagerly awaiting the day when he can get back up there and try again. You don't find that kind of bravery in many adults. It's like too many of us have had our confidence to succeed at the impossible ripped out of our lives. We grew up being taught that it's more helpful to spend all of our time weighing the consequences instead of making them happen. We're led to believe that it makes more sense to focus on fixing how we *might* fail instead of imagining the chance at gaining profit, progress, or prosperity. As a businesswoman, this is entirely counterintuitive. If you start by thinking of all the ways you *might* fail, you will begin working to safeguard yourself against those things rather than staying focused on your goals. Allowing ourselves to see a better outcome automatically eliminates any negative thoughts by default. Our brains can only be occupied with so many things at once. Why not make an effort to fill them with abundance, triumph, and success? What does it cost to hope for good? Ask yourself how much is your happiness worth. Where your mind goes, your actions will follow. Focus on the vision of where you want to end, believe you must get there, and you will find yourself moving every barrier until you finally make it.

## Imagining More

I've been asked what I believe is the most important thing for a successful entrepreneur to have in their arsenal. The answer is simple – envisioning success. Our imaginations are overwhelmingly valuable. Not only do they protect us from crippling fear, but they are the windows to our futures, allowing us the opportunity to see past the hurtful circumstances that can only be relieved with patience. When I focus my imagination on the future, I've found that I can somehow create or manifest the outcome I've pictured. There would be so many days where I wouldn't have a dime to my name, and I'd catch myself hoping to find just a few cents on the ground. I could see myself walking along, looking down, left and right, and finally seeing the money. I could imagine it so clearly that I could literally feel my joy. My heart would start to beat faster, I'd feel warmer, and I'd smile. I could picture myself picking up the money and going to buy food. And it would taste so good. I would feel so peaceful and satisfied. This was the dream I ran in my head every time I had no money or any food. Making money was the practical idea, but most days, all I could think about was tasting something delicious and finishing my day with a full belly. Really, I wanted the food more than anything, but finding the money to buy it seemed more realistic, even if my attention was on the food itself. But then, all of a sudden, like a miracle, I'd come across a mango tree filled with free fruit. A gift practically ready and waiting to be plucked by the same hands I'd imagined eating with only minutes before. Other times, I'd just find the money. Countless moments of my childhood were spent picturing a life that was nothing like my own. I didn't know that it was called manifestation then, but I knew it worked, so I kept doing it. If I wasn't working, then I was resting my feet and keeping my imagination occupied. My why kept me going, but my dreams were my directions because as long as I had an idea of what my end goals looked like, then I'd be able to pinpoint the exact moment when I'd reached them. And life started to reward me for the good things I thought about. Even if the things I wanted didn't always come to me the way I'd thought they would, they'd still turn up somehow and serve the same purpose.

One of the things I would wish for a lot back then, besides money for food and encouragement from adults, was time. It took a lot of time to keep four businesses up and running, and it seemed there just weren't enough hours in the day. If I had more time, then I could find more customers to sell my products to. If there were just a few more hours of daylight, then I could stay out a little later and locate more scrap metal hidden in plain sight. More hours in the morning would mean more opportunities to sell cake and popcorn to people headed to work. If I had free time during the middle of the day, I could pop more popcorn, make more candles, and bake more cakes to sell. As I saw it, the problem was that school took up too much of my time. When I didn't have school, I noticed how much I could get done and how much more money I could make. I knew that school was important for us to do well and give us a better chance at being hired for good jobs, but knowing that didn't make me feel better. School was expensive now, getting a good job later was not a guarantee, and I hated seeing all that money being wasted on something that wasn't a sure profit. I had always gone to premier boarding schools, and after my father died, my mom was adamant that we would continue. Looking back, I know it was because she wanted my sister and I to have all of the advantages she didn't, but at the time, I believed a part of it was to prevent me from staying out late. If I was away at boarding school I'd be somewhere safe, and she would only need to deal with my rebellious nature when I returned home for holidays. We couldn't afford the full tuition at my previous school, so my mom ended up finding a school that would take the two of us girls on a type of scholarship. The school was situated far away in the countryside, sponsored by a Greek organization that allowed orphaned children like us to attend at a fraction of the cost. With our 70% discount, we had enough funds to go, but there was still travel and uniforms, and both of those added up fast. My mom wanted to help with tuition, but barely two terms in, we were being sent home over and over again because she hadn't paid. Each time we were sent home meant I'd have to find a way to come up with the extra money to pay for our transportation back. Knowing exactly how hard it was to earn enough pennies to buy a meal made the cost of transportation seem all the more like a wasteful and useless expense. It was so clear to me but impossible to explain to my mother in a way that she'd understand what I was seeing. I decided that this boarding school arrangement made no sense and would be short-lived. I wasn't sure how, but I was certain I could bring it to an end.

Sewage contamination from the floodwaters that frequently accumulated across Uganda kept my sister and I sick with Typhoid regularly. One particular time she got so sick when we were away at school they wouldn't permit us to go home. For about a week, the school nurse insisted that she keep my sister with her, even though I demanded a pass to take her with me.

She wasn't even a real nurse anyway. "I'm not giving it to her because I can treat her," she said. This woman didn't even have any medical training! She'd gone through the same program for newly graduated high school students who had an interest in becoming a medical professional. Far from a doctor, she was more like a Certified Nursing Assistant (CNA), and even that's saying a lot. The days passed, and my sister was getting no better. I could see that this "nurse" was grossly overestimating her skill set. One day, I visited my sister to check on her, and the woman was trying to hook her up to a saline drip for her dehydration. It was clear she had no idea what she was doing. I wasn't exactly sure of what the right way looked like, but every time she pierced my sister, she would squirm and cry. The nurse juggled a handful of needles in her hands without a clue of how to handle them while my sister was screaming at the top of her lungs begging for it all to end. I watched her stab at my sister's arm at least nine times, only to take the needle out again and again because it had missed the mark. My sister was obviously in agony, but I knew I needed to remain quiet and respectful. However, after the tenth time, something in me exploded.

"You have absolutely no idea what you're doing, do you?" I shouted. "You didn't even go to school for this. You know, you should be able to find the vein within like, three tries. What is this? Try number ten? You're not even a real nurse!" I had started with a yell, but by the time I finished, I was absolutely screeching. It didn't matter that my sister was deathly ill and I was scared of losing her. It didn't matter that the adult responsible for keeping her alive was clearly and frighteningly incompetent. It was not acceptable for a student to speak to a school official as I had. That kind of disrespect carried a hefty punishment. The administration almost immediately sentenced me to something like cleaning toilets. I refused. If anything, they should have thanked me for putting that woman in her place. For this, I was suspended for a week. I was sent home immediately, along with my sister, who did make a full recovery once she got back home. When the week was up, I went back to school, this time with my mom by my side. But at my return, the punishment was even more severe. I don't even remember the full details, but basically, they wanted to get the entire school together for an assembly and beat me in front of everyone. Apparently they'd already planned the assembly, but since I was just coming home from suspension they thought it would be a perfect time to make an example out of me. We tried to convince them that my suspension was punishment enough, but still they insisted. It didn't help that we were behind on tuition either. That just made them even more motivated to humiliate me. But there was no way I was going to allow them to touch me. No one would beat me, embarrass me, or diminish me. My mother agreed, we left, and I refused to go back. We also couldn't afford to pay what we owed, and I couldn't return without balancing the books anyway, so it wasn't likely that I would return anytime soon. The entire ordeal was more of an annoyance than anything, but I didn't have to go to boarding school from that point on. I hadn't known how it would happen, but it was exactly what I'd hoped for.

    With the time constraints of boarding school lifted, I was free to focus on my businesses and sharpen my vision of what I wanted my future to be. On days when I had no money and no food, I would lay in bed with my empty stomach dreaming of the day I would have chicken. But not just one chicken, a table full of chicken prepared in every way I could imagine. The whole table was covered in so much chicken that I couldn't eat it all. I could taste the different types, feel the different textures as I bit in, smell the seasonings, and feel the oil and liquid on my fingers as I ate. And then I pictured feeling happy and satisfied with the knowledge that I would buy and eat just as much chicken the next day and every day for the rest of my life. A bit older now, I was getting accustomed to envisioning myself beyond a few pennies on the ground or a tree full of ripe mangoes. Now, I could picture myself having more than I ever imagined before. In my neighborhood there was a girl who had been to London, and I would sit and listen to her talk for hours about life there. I began to envision myself there shopping, riding the bus, and walking in the streets. I was going to restaurants buying food anytime I wanted, had money in my pocket, and was living an altogether different life. I could picture it so clearly that I could feel the air, smell the city, and hear the noise. My imagination took me to the place I wanted to be in the future, which made my path to getting there so clear. I could see myself leaving Uganda and traveling to London, stepping out into the city, and feeling not a shred of fear or uncertainty as I looked around, ready for what came next.

My imagination sustained me when we had nothing at all, keeping my mind gratified with happy images of a better future. It kept me satiated when I hoped for *matoke*[2] and got *posho*, or

---

[2] Matoke is a savory, traditional Ugandan dish composed of mashed plantain. Matoke was a dish that my family could only have if my mom would travel upcountry or someone we knew was coming from that way and they'd bring plantains back with them. It wasn't much, but it was better than most of the other things we could afford.

when I wished for meat to have with the matoke and got no more food for another however many days. I didn't mind silverfish with peanut sauce, but they were very tiny fish, barely larger than a sardine or anchovy. Rather than getting lost in sadness over the lack of meat on their bones, and mine, I chose to get caught up in the thought of being able to pick my favorite piece of chicken out of the dinner that I knew I'd someday be able to buy for us. It just made more sense for me to give my undivided attention to the things I wanted. Strengthening our imaginative abilities can do wonders for our lives, but just like gratitude, it takes practice. Since I've been doing it so long, it's easy for me to just think of what I'm working toward, but for many others, it helps to write it down like in a list of goals or map it out on a vision board. Devoting our time to becoming more specific and pointed with our thoughts can only help us in the long run. Visualizing something other than what we're presented with is tremendously beneficial when we're trying to escape that same thing physically. If I had denied my imagination and accepted the life that the world was giving me, I have no doubts that I wouldn't be anywhere near where I am today. When I chose to look at the world for what it could give me, opposed to what I had, I'd unknowingly unlocked a secret to success. If you can see it, then you can reach it.

 A perfect way to strengthen your imagination is by thinking intently about your favorite thing. Whatever it is that makes you smile, think about it. If it's your favorite food, then try to envision every single detail of the meal you would have. Imagine all the smells that would fill your nostrils and the room in which the dish is prepared and served. Think of the temperature of the servings.

Pretend to feel the weight in your hand as you prepare to lift it toward your mouth. What does the plate feel like in your hands? Or is it a bowl that you're eating out of? Maybe it's pizza, so you use your hands. Is there any grease dripping down your fingers or cheese oozing down your wrist? Taste the flavors that you know and love. Is the texture of this food crispy or soft? Does each bite melt in your mouth, or does it take some work to dissolve between your teeth? It can be a lot of work, but once you do it a few times, it becomes much easier to let your mind lead you to wonderful places. Very soon, it becomes strong enough to imagine never before seen images and experiences, thus giving rise to new perspectives and an entirely new life.

As much as I appreciated where I was and what I had, I was much more concerned with where I was going. But I had complete and total confidence that as long as I stayed focused and kept moving toward my vision, I'd get there sooner or later. Focusing on the appealing results of my side hustles became my best defense against all the things that could have stopped me from reaching my goals. Because we can use our imaginations to travel to far away places, we can use them to lift our spirits, even use them to inform our present decisions. But unfortunately, we cannot use them to alter time. No matter how much I wished to be older so I could have all the things I saw in my head, I still had to wait to have them, and there was no telling when that would be. As the days continued to slowly pass by and I was still getting removed from school and teased relentlessly by my classmates for being poor, I lived my life and ran my businesses on repeat. I made it a point to adopt those consistent behaviors that could persistently end in positive outcomes. I appreciated where I was, but I was much more concerned with where I was going. I supposed that as long as I followed the steps to getting rich – making money, saving money, then investing it to make more – I'd eventually get everything I wanted. And as I waited some time for my life to finally change for the better, meditating on the idea that I would someday meet my dreams became more crucial with time.

# CHAPTER 3

# Longing For An Illusion

### A lesson on patience, persistence, and pushing past fear

When I was eight years old, I had this dream I still remember so vividly to this day. In the dream, I'd been flying. And at that point, I didn't even know how to swim in real life, but in the dream that's exactly how I was flying. Not really flying like a bird, but swimming like one would in a pool or body of water. I was asleep, but my dream body was soaring amongst the clouds, gliding effortlessly through the air. At the beginning of the dream, I was being bullied by some kids in the schoolyard. They were brutally teasing me, laughing at me, and humiliating me. One in particular had been chasing me. Figuring since it was my dream in the first place, I decided to take off. I stopped running away, and I started to fly as if it were the most natural and logical thing in the world to do. I quickly rose and glided away like I'd been doing it all my life. No fear, no contemplation, just easy floating. Soon, I was so high up that the kids looked much smaller than they were before, all of them much less intimidating than they'd been a few short moments ago. It was funny because when I was on the ground, they'd been so vicious, but all of a sudden they were watching me sail across the clear blue sky with envy painted across their faces. I could instantly see their newfound admiration for me was soured by the guilt of doubting someone who could fly. Those deeply satisfying feelings of joy, accomplishment, and freedom automatically burned a mark on my heart and soul that I've carried with me always.

In Uganda, dream interpretation is a big thing. As in many cultures, we believe that important messages and information come to us through dreams. Many of us wake up from our dreams, desperately hoping to find answers to what they mean. Maybe we've received a sign from God on what we should do next with our careers. Or, it could be a warning. Maybe we're suffering from some unknown illness that our bodies are trying to relate to us through these phantom fantasies. Whatever information can be found is believed to always help navigate life in the real world. My dream was so powerful, so vivid, and so overwhelming that I was sure it meant something important. Looking for an answer, I found an article in the newspaper that finally explained my vision. The article stated that if you ever have a dream of flying, it means you are destined for greatness. Flying above buildings and homes, maybe even reaching the clouds and then surpassing them, was what the article said to be a clear sign the dreamer will be above others. Symbolically, this dream represented the ascent of a superior leader. After reading this, I was convinced. I was born to be great. And though I was the only one who'd seen it, this dream was my proof. I was destined for greatness and no one on the planet could tell me differently.

## Life Goes On

By the time I was 12 years old, my life still hadn't reflected the interpretation, but the dream of my overcoming never left me. I'd still believed with all my heart that even if my father was no longer around and money was much harder to come by, I would still be great. Unfortunately, it seemed like I was the only one who truly believed that. In hindsight, everyone else around me was the problem, but that didn't keep their thoughts from affecting my feelings. I was the only one with a clear mind, the only one who had a true understanding of my destiny and a picture that painted my success. Everyone else just saw the little girl I was, growing up in a poor country without a father and the odds stacked up against her. They never once suspended their beliefs of what I was supposed to be, nor did they make room in their minds for who I could become. I was a kid who worked hard. I had four successful enterprises, was making money, being endlessly resourceful and dedicated beyond my years, but to most people I was just disobedient and rebellious. It was easier for them to put me into a predictable box. Then they could move on with their own lives and the obstacles they routinely faced themselves. I knew I couldn't blame anyone for not believing in me and my dreams, but realizing that truth didn't necessarily make things any easier. It was a continuous internal struggle for me. How can you believe in yourself when no one else does?

Every day I fiercely imagined a new life in the midst of working multiple hustles. I found retreating into my mind helped to reinvigorate me as time passed as slowly as it wanted. We were barely making ends meet. To cope with the harsh realities I was facing, I escaped to the place where I was powerful, successful, and in control. I traveled to a place where there was no uncertainty, no limits, and no hunger. Daydreaming of driving around in my nice car with my kids as we went shopping as a family made me smile when I wanted to cry. I could feel the excitement as if this time was real and near. I'd lay down at night watching movies play on the screen of my mind, showcasing lavish Christmases with two freshly slaughtered cows for our entire extended family to enjoy. These cows were provided by me, exactly the same way my father used to do. I was anxiously looking forward to these moments that felt so close, with certainty the way a child looks forward to their birthday. But in the present, my life continued to drag forward, and I plodded along with it.

I was turning reasonable profits through my four enterprises, but it wasn't anything substantial enough to get us out of the ghetto. Although I knew the path I was on was the right one, sometimes it felt like I was killing myself, working just to stay alive. The constant pressure to make money for food and everyday expenses was still there. Despite my successful escape from boarding school, affording my tuition was still a challenge. In Uganda, if you cannot afford to pay tuition, you simply do not go to school. To not attend school would have brought me to a level even lower than we were. And my family's constant struggle with our school finances made me an easy target for the other poor kids who could afford just a bit more than we could.

To sum it up, I hated school. And not because I wasn't smart or couldn't handle the work, but because I was poor. Students, teachers, and school administrators alike looked down on me. I never really wanted to go, but I always understood the value of getting a good education, so I made school a reluctant priority. I assumed I could keep up my side hustles to help us eat and live day-to-day. That would help me finish school and fulfill my dreams of becoming a lawyer. Once I became a lawyer, then I'd have enough money to buy my mom a house, food, a car, and whatever else she might need or ever want. To accomplish that, I was willing to put up with almost anything, even if it made me want to quit altogether. For instance, take my grades. As far as I know, I did very well in school, but I never had concrete evidence to show it. It wasn't that the schools didn't issue report cards. It was just that not everybody got one. For those of us behind on tuition, we'd never get to see our grades. Because my family was always behind on tuition, for me, report cards became like a fantasy.

Report card day became just another way I was reminded of my position in the world and all of the stigmas my disadvantages carried. While the other students compared grades, talked about their standing and admired each other, I was on the sideline. Everyone could see I had no report card, and everyone knew why. But it was not my nature to fall victim to circumstances I could not change or let myself wallow in the unfairness of it all. For me, the bigger issue was that I needed the feedback to gauge how I was doing in school so I could do better. Not receiving my report card made getting that information more challenging. But instead of letting my emotions take over, I thought of a workaround. If I wanted to tell how I was doing in school, I would have to pay close attention to my friends. I began trying my best to keep track of my remarks each term, and I would test my knowledge against the people whose progress I knew of for sure. This way, I could gauge exactly where I fell and not be left completely in the dark about my standings. Depending on how well another person did, I could get an idea of how well I'd done. *On that assignment I got an 80. If they got a 70 and that person got a 90, then I must've done pretty well.* My self-assessment system didn't make report card day any less socially painful, but it did help my sanity as I made my way toward my life goals.

Another reason school was, in general, a terrible experience for me was because I was always *the new kid*. From the time my dad died until I reached secondary school in my teenage years, I had to switch schools every time there was a tuition bill we could not pay. And this happened all the time. In Uganda, there are three terms in each school year, like semesters - first term, second term, third. Some years, I went to three different schools because I couldn't afford to be admitted for the next term. If there was a balance for the previous term, there was usually no way we'd be able to afford that on top of the installments for the new term. Starting a clean slate somewhere else was the only way to resolve this dilemma. And everyone knew it. Starting a new school every semester is a sign that you're so poor you can't even afford to consistently go to school. So the new kid is not just the poor kid, but the *very* poor kid. Most people living in my area were poor, but the poorer you were, the worse you were treated by everyone else. But this is not something unique to Uganda. It's something that happens all the time, all over the world. It's a social hierarchy that constantly plays itself out. There are just some people who need to belittle others just so they can feel better about themselves. I felt great about myself, so I guess there were plenty of kids who felt like they needed to bring me back down to earth. I was consistently teased, bullied, and embarrassed by the other kids. And that was just the half of it. In addition to being the new kid each term, I was also always being sent home because my tuition bill wasn't paid. Rarely was this handled privately or respectfully to preserve my feelings or save me from embarrassment. Students who had unpaid tuition were forced to do extra work like cleaning toilets and other odd jobs around campus, so those things I had to do regularly became another form of daily public shaming. By my high school years, I started to use the time I had to be there more to my advantage, doing favors for the lazy rich kids in exchange for sugar for my porridge or any kind of small snack they could spare. These kids would show up to school with a suitcase full of snacks and a crazy amount of pocket money, and if I was smart about it, I could figure out ways to get them to give me what they had. In time, I built a customer base at my high school and started a type of personal support business, doing their work and washing their uniforms. But no matter how useful I was, kids were still cruel. I might've been getting something out of them in return, but they never respected me and that was difficult to cope with.

Despite rarely getting to see my grades and working long hours outside of school every day, I still managed to get my assignments done, arrive at school on time, and be courteous to my classmates and administrators. These traits made me appealing for student leadership roles, and I got picked often. Sometimes I would be the class monitor, watching over all the students if the teacher had to leave, taking over lessons and reporting back to them everything we finished when they returned. Other times, I got to be the information minister, which I really liked. That meant I'd report the administration's news to the student body during assemblies and write articles with news bits or pieces about what had gone on during the weekends. I was even chosen to be the head girl, which meant I had multiple responsibilities. One of them was disciplining the other kids or reporting them to the administration if they broke the rules. Every day, I'd wake up at 5 a.m., walk 3 miles to school, and wait at the front gate for the kids who came in after the bell. If by some chance I woke up later than usual, I'd take the mini-bus to get there faster and on time because I cared so much about my position. A measure of respect should've come with being named head girl, but when I'd issue a reprimand or discipline to someone arriving late, they'd often make a comment to insult me. *I don't have to listen to you. You're the head girl that doesn't pay tuition.* As much as their disdain hurt, I knew school was a means to an end. Like my businesses, it was a necessary but difficult step I had to take to get to where I was going. While I was there, I would just need to learn what I could.

School became a place where I stuck out for all the wrong reasons. For a long time, I only had two dresses. I'd wash one, wear the other while it dried, and do it all over again the next day and every day after. I wasn't popular like the cool kids with money and nice clothing because I had nothing for the other kids to want. It made me lonely and vulnerable, and unfortunately, there were adults who not only allowed it, but tried to take advantage of it. One particular situation is especially painful to recall. I had a teacher that I felt very close to just before I reached secondary school. I was 13 years old then and studying for the exams that would help place me in high school. They were basically the exams that wrapped up my primary school years, so they were important. This teacher to me was special, always very nice and encouraging. He'd advocated for my sister and me when we couldn't make our tuition installments, trying to prevent school officials from sending us home. He'd also give me a lot of responsibility in class, which I believed was because I was smart and an excellent student. For the whole school year he was my teacher, I felt a sense of stability and certainty, unlike the previous years that had been so difficult. This man was my favorite teacher and the first person who I believed had the same confidence in me that I had in myself. But when we did our final exams, these feelings went completely out the window.

The exams I'm referring to are like the first step into getting into serious academics. Their results turn you into an adult, dictating your learning and playing a role in the schools you were going to be able to attend later on in life and at what level you'd be educated. I needed to become a lawyer so these exams were extremely important to me. The day before I took them, I received a phone call from my favorite teacher. Because he was so supportive and encouraging of my dream to be a lawyer, it didn't raise any red flags for me when he called to check-in. He was away in another city monitoring a different school's exams as teachers were obligated to do. He'd called another teacher and told them to give me a pass to take the call outside of school so we could speak privately. I didn't really know what to expect, but I trusted him, so I initially felt okay with having the conversation. When we first started speaking, it was lighthearted and business as usual. Even though it was out of the ordinary for him to be calling, it made sense to me that he would be checking in on me, his favorite student, at a critical time in my education. If he weren't in town, he would be checking with me during school.

"How are you? Are you ready for the exams tomorrow? Are you excited?" He asked. I answered positively, feeling so special and validated. "I have so much faith that you're going to do really well. I feel like I've helped you a lot during this whole year," he continued. I agreed. I told him how much I appreciated everything he'd done. I'd felt truly grateful, and I sincerely thanked him. He'd been the first person to treat me as someone of value since my father. He recognized my worth, and he believed that I'd do well. When he looked at me, he didn't see a worthless girl. He saw the person who could fly in her dreams. Having that was like a crack of light in the dark. Then suddenly, the call turned.

"So when you're done with your exams, are you going to bring me a 'thank you' chicken for all of the help I've given you?" His request caught me off guard. I couldn't tell at first if he was being light-hearted and teasing harmlessly or being sincere. I'd never visited his house, seen him outside of school, or even been alone with him. However, in our culture a chicken is usually presented as a form of gratitude and respect. When you visit someone's house, you can bring a chicken to show how thankful you are for the invitation and how much you appreciate their hospitality. Knowing this fact, I politely agreed, even though I was starting to feel a bit uncomfortable. But that was precisely the answer he needed to show his true colors.

"Well, are you going to bring me just the chicken or your whole body?" He asked. I was speechless. I felt my stomach clench, a warmth climb from my chest up to my neck and spread across my face. My mouth and throat were instantly dry, so it was difficult for me to form words. I told him I didn't know about that, but he kept going. Kept pressing for me to meet him in the city after exams, pushing for us to sneak away and spend some alone time together. It was disturbing and one of the biggest disappointments of my life. Somehow I ended the call and tried to get back to my studying, but it was nearly impossible. I remember laying down that night feeling so confused, ashamed, and crushed, thinking, 'how can I do these determining exams tomorrow when I can barely concentrate on reading tonight?' It was all a sad reminder of my circumstances. Even though I'd begun to view things differently, life outside of my head stayed the same. I was only 13 years old, but this grown man, a prominent authority figure in my life, viewed me the way he wanted to. I fit his perceptions of a poor girl from my neighborhood, either meant to be a wife or a prostitute and not much else. This teacher had given me hope that there were people who would see my value and my potential, and the loss of that hope felt like losing air to breathe. This person was not special. He was the same as my auntie, extended family, neighbors, and everyone around me. It was so weird, and it's something I don't think I'll ever forget. As painful as this moment was, it was another valuable lesson that changed my understanding of the world and how people operate in it. I had so many fantastic dreams that played on the screen of my mind all day, every day, that sometimes it seemed like I was living with my head in the clouds. If I wasn't focused on my schoolwork or side hustle strategies, I was looking toward a brighter future for myself. But that day I learned all at once, those dreams were all my own and my journey toward them was shaping up to be a lonely one.

## Success Breeds Respect, But Persistence Is Required

Looking back, the most valuable things I learned at school were not things I learned in the classroom. I saw the way other students treated me because I was poor. I recognized a change in how they treated me when they realized my services were valuable to them. I saw what happened when you have authority but not respect. And just how much of yourself you give when you trust, and how greatly you could be taken advantage of when you did. These were all life lessons that moved me miles ahead. I was beginning to figure the world out, and fewer and fewer things were confusing to me. The more I thought about the incident with my teacher, the more I was motivated to move forward. I had come to rely on this person and appreciate him for validating my worth. But he wasn't trying to build me up. He was trying to take something from me. From that moment on, I would never confuse the two again. Further considering our own family had abandoned us made me long for a life of success and a lasting position of authority. When my father was alive, he was the man around town that so many people loved, and most importantly, respected. I'd never been able to imagine anyone talking to him in any tone that wasn't pleasing. I couldn't fathom people ignoring him like they did me or outwardly questioning his decisions, as that was becoming a common occurrence in my life. It never crossed my mind to think if anyone ever made such gross assumptions about my father like my teacher had done with me. People treated us so harshly simply because we didn't have a lot. That made me think much harder about what other things I could gain from the prosperity I hoped to eventually have, and slowly, the wheels in my brain began turning.

I thought about what life in our city looked like for the people in my shoes compared to those who could afford as many shoes as they'd liked. Life seemed much easier for them, almost like they paid everyone they encountered to treat them nicely. I noticed that if you were successful, everyone craved your attention and did whatever they could to get it. They went out of their way to smile at you and speak to you so they could ask about your life and business and bask in the glory of your perfect decisions. Almost like they were hoping that knowing you or having contact with you would somehow benefit them. People always wanted to know how you were doing and what you had, and as soon as you revealed it to them, they'd always say they wished they'd done the same or had whatever it was you did. Successful people were always seen as intelligent and full of wisdom. Apparently because of this, successful people were believed to rarely make mistakes, so they were passionately trusted. And anyone as remarkable as this was not ever to be treated harshly, lest you wanted to get on their bad side. Successful people were those who you wanted to be on your side, so it would be helpful for you to get on their good one. Successful people had power, which meant they had the means to make your life much better than you could if you were trying to do it alone. Remembering all the people who reached out to our family with well wishes after my father died, and all the others who treated us like dirt once they realized his money and power were gone, it finally made sense to me. Anyone who had success had respect.

Here in the real world, we rate success by what people finish, not what they start. If your dream is to one day open and own your own restaurant, but the only thing you do is have the idea, then it's physically impossible for you to ever reach what you've dreamt of. To achieve your dreams, you have to complete what you started when you imagined a specific outcome for your future. To turn fantasies into reality, you have to turn that energy into action and then keep it going. And you can never stop until you've created the thing in which you've only been able to imagine. Because in life, people don't fail to achieve their dreams – they just quit too soon. Persistence is the proof that you've been victorious. Each time you choose to persevere and continue doing whatever it is you think will bring you your desires, you have escaped defeat. Your prize for winning this battle is the bliss of being that much closer to what you've been waiting for. Success can only be found by those who hold on long after others have let go.

When measuring anything, we count only what we can see and not what *could* be there. You would never say that you have built the tallest building in the world, but only have a 10-foot model to show for it. If you were asked to create a 10-foot model of a skyscraper by whoever you presented your work to, then by their standards, you were successful. But what about yours? If you're never clear on what you actually want to achieve, then it'll never be yours because technically, there is nothing to have. If I wanted to have the most success, I needed a concrete way to measure it. Money quickly became the obvious choice for me. The older I got, the more I understood how money ran the world we lived in. Having money was necessary for meeting life's most basic needs. Where I was from, if you wanted to make it from one day to the next with your heart still beating, then you needed to either have money or know someone who would share theirs with you. If you had a lot of money, that meant you could spend less time trying to make enough to survive and spend more time actually living and enjoying the rest of what life had to offer. Sadly, everyone can't afford to pay the price for what life has to offer, but that didn't mean anything to me because I planned on it. Thinking of what money I'd made and considering some of the things I'd picked up along the way concerning rich people and their lifestyles, I tallied up the exact dollar amount I thought would be the marker for my success. I decided that once I'd earned one million dollars, I'd know for sure that I was successful. Once I had that much money, I would definitely be able to do all the things I imagined daily. But a million dollars was so much money. I had trouble visualizing what that many bills would look like, so I replaced that picture with what I believed to be a million-dollar lifestyle. Having a number to look for completely solidified my vision, and in turn, my journey toward it. It gave me a definite beginning and ending to the road that would be called a success by anyone who came across it. And that number also gave me the ambition and determination to continue striving through many, many difficult years.

## Holding On To Virtues

I had a limited number of hours available each day, and I knew how much money I could make in one of those hours if I properly focused my attention toward one or more of my businesses.

Every hour I wasn't working was an hour I wasn't making money to put back into my business to make more. The biggest barrier by far was the never-ending need to find food and simply survive. I understood how each hour spent working or looking for food was setting me further back from reaching my life goals. So as I continued working to make money, how I gained the things I needed grew to become much more sophisticated.

The ghetto where we lived was very close to a mosque. I'm not Muslim, but their place of worship became a source of rescue during my childhood. During the season of Ramadan, observant practitioners of the Islamic faith fast each day from dawn until sunset. It is a sacred and deeply purposeful ritual requiring a commendable commitment to religious tradition. Each day, my Muslim friends and neighbors at the mosque would break their fast at dusk with a large, hearty meal, which the mosque would prepare and serve for free. Gathering together in celebration of their obedience and perseverance for the day, they'd strengthen themselves in preparation for the next. Driven first by starvation and second by my inability to pass up a great opportunity, each year, I would pretend to be Muslim for the whole month of Ramadan. This way, I could visit the mosque and receive the free food they gave away for anyone breaking their fast with them. Wearing a niqab[3] and going by a Muslim name I'd given myself, I'd rush over every day of that month to help prep the food for later when everyone would be back to break their fasts. Very early in the morning, I'd be there, offering to do anything and everything to be helpful.

---

3 A garment of clothing worn by some Muslim women that covers the face leaving only the eyes uncovered.

Whatever was asked of me, I would obey, always remaining on my absolute best behavior. Each evening, I would be entrusted to help serve the food, which was exactly what I needed to get what I wanted.

During Ramadan, the meals at the mosque were usually a combination of rice and meat that they'd put into small bags. At dusk, we would hand them out to visitors. Because I was so obedient and helpful, no one ever doubted me when I told them people hadn't received their meals. If I told them some on the north side of the mosque hadn't eaten yet, they'd give me a few more bags to take out and distribute. Once that happened, I'd run over to my nephew, who I'd have standing near the back of the building, hand him the bags of food to hold onto, and then keep doing so until we'd collected enough for us to take home and have dinner with everyone in our family. Though I never became a Muslim nor followed the religion, that ritual became my Ramadan tradition. Each year as the holy month approached, I would feel the weight on my shoulders lighten. I knew for one glorious month, I would not have to worry about how we would survive. Each day I went to the mosque, I knew I would be fed, and I was so completely grateful for that shred of certainty.

Being around the mosque at that time is one of the fondest memories I have of my childhood, despite not ever having observed the religion. While the Islamic followers looked forward to being brought closer to heaven through fasting, we looked forward to full bellies. Food was my heaven. It was my safe space and the thing that instantly let me know that everything was alright once it hit my tongue. At a time when things were changing so fast and almost not at all, food was both my peace and my prime mover. I knew it was the only thing I needed to survive long enough to meet my goals, so whenever I ate anything, I'd savor every bite in deep appreciation. And if food was my heaven, then making money became my meditation, an exercise and practice through which salvation could be revealed. But making enough money to meet my success was going to require a great deal of patience.

Early on, I'd learned to cherish the practice of gratitude, but that was the first of many of life's virtues I'd found, which made getting by a whole lot easier. If persistence is a requirement for accomplishing what you hope for, then patience is something you need to keep yourself from going crazy while waiting to have what you've been working for. I'd seen firsthand the benefits of patience when I interacted with the people at the mosque. They wouldn't eat a single thing all day long, and they'd do it for a whole month willingly, and in most cases, happily. I knew from my own experience with hunger that they were in pain, weak, tired, and irritable. But they didn't show it. They knew the discomfort was temporary, that it was a part of the bigger and better picture. Their hunger was something inevitable they chose and would simply need to endure until it ended. They were patient in waiting for the sun to set just as I was learning to be patient while I waited to make my million dollars.

I recognized and accepted every dollar I made couldn't be saved. I knew if I wanted to be successful, I needed to be patient and have faith in the slow build. This recognition helped me persist whenever I felt like I'd never be able to keep going. Each time I felt like giving up, my understanding and practice of patience pushed me when my why was not enough. When the lights kept going out, and the house continued to flood at 2 a.m., and I was repeatedly expelled from school for being unable to pay my tuition, my patience helped me to avoid making irrational decisions. It reminded me that my day of success would come, so waiting for it was not all that bad. Because the passage of time is inevitable, but our patience is not. That part is a choice. When things begin to seem unbearable, we might resort to doing the wrong things for the wrong reasons, like taking naive shortcuts to accomplish our goals. In business, this might mean cutting corners and creating a bad product that loses revenue. If I hadn't remained patient as I persisted in my pursuit of riches, I could have done any number of things that would've gotten me hurt, killed, or totally derailed simply because I was trying to speed up the process. Learning patience and perseverance kept me from derailing myself as a businesswoman countless times. One does not need to be patient to receive the things you've put in the effort to chase. However, remaining calm with your heart firmly rooted in the knowledge that what you long for the most will eventually reach you is a precious ability that shouldn't be taken for granted. Some of my greatest business successes were the direct result of my ability to draw on my patience.

    Another part of me that really began to shine during this time was my generosity. Watching my Muslim friends and neighbors come together, treating each other with kindness, encouraging others to take food first and offering their own was an enlightening experience. They were willing to go without for the benefit of others, this was all part of the spirit of Ramadan. I was surrounded by people who felt good by making others feel good. Witnessing generosity in action each night at the mosque flooded me with memories of my father. I remembered dozens of examples of his generosity, which taught me the beauty behind giving, and the secret that it isn't entirely unselfish to serve others. With all the people he was supporting, it was undeniable that he was a vastly wealthy man. He had more than enough for himself, so he shared as much as he wanted with everyone else. When you show people generosity, they feel like they owe you. This is something that consequently brings more prosperity into your life. Even if the only thing returned is simply love and respect, it's still a kindness multiplied and gratefully received when it comes back to the giver. Additionally, no one makes it on their own. The more you're willing to help others, the more they're willing to help you. Regardless of your needs, you can likely count on who you've been there for to do the same for you.

    I was always grateful for the people at the mosque who were so open with their generosity. And when I really began to think about it, I was thankful for so many others. I remembered a teacher who generally showed my sister and me mercy, helping us when we needed it because he'd known our father when he owned a farm in the man's hometown. He'd thought highly of my father and showed us kindness even when some teachers and administrators refused to. Also, I didn't have to deal with the same unwanted attention I'd received from my former favorite teacher with this man. I thought about how thankful I was for the people that bought what I had to sell. Without them, I could have never survived how I learned how or cultivated the basics of entrepreneurship which ultimately made me a millionaire. Each time my customers gave me money, it was an act of pure generosity. I was happy they enjoyed paying for the convenience I offered with my items more than the items themselves. Possibly, they could have gotten the things I was selling from someplace else at a different time, but instead they chose to support me. They were acting from a place of kindness when they bought from me and made an important choice that benefitted my family. Whether that choice was conscious or not wasn't at all significant in the grand scheme of things. Their giving, whether purposeful or frivolous, was making a significant difference in my life. Every chance I got, I gave. I knew what it felt like to be on the receiving end, and that was a feeling I believed everyone should be able to experience.

Generosity, I learned, was something that you could give, even if you had very little yourself. If you made another person's needs important enough to you, eventually you would find a way to bring something kind and meaningful to their world. Even when I didn't have much, I always used to help. During our last year of primary school, I had a friend who ended up on the receiving end of this generosity. To move on to high school, she needed a total of 100,000 shillings[4] to take her qualifying exams - 50,000 shillings for tuition and 50,000 for registration! Even with my multiple businesses and streams of income, this was a lot of money, and I struggled to scrape together what I needed to cover my own education. But she was a dear friend, and I didn't have many of those

---

[4] The shilling is the official currency of Uganda. As of June 2020, 1 US dollar was equivalent to approximately 3,700 shillings after decades of inflation and rapid economic growth.

at the time. If she could not get the money she needed to move on to high school, she would end up wasting the four years of Uganda's equivalent to junior high school. I could not bear the thought or the unfairness of her situation. I knew how much I was struggling, but her family was too, and without any possible source of income, it wasn't likely they'd be able to afford what she needed. And so I jumped into action. Staying home for two weeks to sell popcorn around the clock, I'd made enough money to cover all her expenses. I hadn't even finished paying off my own tuition, but I was driven to solve this problem for her, knowing it would also mean I had the power to solve my own troubles. I was able to earn enough for us both, and in the decades since, her love, support, and loyal friendship have been repaid one hundred times over.

Another time, I met a lady who had just moved with her family to our neighborhood from Congo. She was pregnant and had other young children who were adorable! They melted my heart. One afternoon when I was selling popcorn, she asked for some, explaining she didn't have enough money to pay. Her husband was looking for a job but hadn't found one yet. Once he did, she promised she'd come back to give me what she owed. It had been some time since she'd had food, and I felt so worried for her and her unborn baby. It hurt to think about how much she must have been suffering. How helpless she must have felt knowing no one, having no one to help, and worrying so much about whether her child would survive. I just remember thinking about how we'd steal food from the palace and how easy it would be to swipe extra for her and the kids. I told her to take all the popcorn she needed, and I promised, anytime I got food, I would also try to get her some. For the next month, every single time I got food for myself and my household, I made sure to take that woman some. By the end of the month, that family ended up moving to a different city. I never saw them again, but I knew for sure I'd made a meaningful difference in their lives, and that made me feel good.

Gratitude, creativity, patience, and generosity were some of the major things that made my journey to success that much more fulfilling. It didn't take me very long to streamline my entrepreneurial process, but it did take a long time for me to see any considerable results. However, all the days I woke up wishing for more rest or when my whole body would ache from working it so many hours without nourishment, I persisted. Or any other times I felt like relaxing my efforts, those were the days I employed tricks that helped me endure the monotony of being consistent.

Gratitude kept me grounded in the present, affirming all the progress I'd made since losing my father. Creativity helped me to go further than what I could see in front of me and use my resources in imaginative ways, giving me the means to create an existence from the amazing images that played in my mind. Patience helped me keep my cool as I counted the days until I could finally receive my degree and begin living an easy, comfortable life. Being kind and giving to people has always been something I really cared about and loved to do. Practicing generosity gave me a chance to have some joy for myself – a rare blessing in my life that was suddenly filled with so many grave responsibilities. Had I not held onto these forgiving properties of life, I'm not sure where I'd be. If I wasn't focused on the finer things, then my greatest obsession with wanting to leave Uganda would have never been realized, and I might still be living there.

## Looking To London

Living near the mosque and being a seasonal participant in their traditions meant I had the opportunity to get to know some of the Muslim families in our community. This one family, in particular, lived very close to us, and I thought they led a good life. They had daughters who were always dressed nicely, and on holidays I'd watch them pass by our house carrying all these delicious dishes for their family. At that time, I worked a great deal, walking around selling whatever it was I was selling, and I was at a low point in school. I knew our Muslim neighbors had a daughter who lived in London, but she'd moved away long before we came to the community. Their family was also very private, so I didn't know much about their lives. Nonetheless, I assumed if they had a daughter living successfully enough in Europe, then it meant she probably had the means to send money back home to her family in Uganda. This was not the wild assumption of an imaginative child either. In fact, it was a reasonable conclusion to draw. Generally, it seemed most people who moved out of the country to places like the United Kingdom or the United States would get to those places, start working, and send money back home to build houses for their parents and become notable providers for their households. For a common family to prosper in Uganda during that time, it was almost necessary for someone to leave and establish themselves elsewhere while still helping their family make ends meet.

In Uganda, the current president has been in power for nearly 35 years now, ruling a military dictatorship based on tribalism. Before I was born until now, as the president ascended to power and ran the country, he filled any and all key positions in his cabinet with people from his tribe. Anyone who was not a member of the president's tribe simply didn't have the opportunity to prosper. This tribalism has trickled down through every level of the population. In addition to this, there just aren't any jobs to be had by anyone, regardless of tribal heritage. Many kids go to school, graduate, and have no options for employment, let alone a pathway to a sustainable career. If they can find employment, it generally isn't anywhere near what they went to school for. And for those lucky enough to get hired, an employed position rarely guarantees good pay.

In a country where money is scarce, and opportunities are slim, it's hard to find people you can trust. Most times, if you are dealing with anyone you tend to know them really well – either they grew up in your neighborhood or belonged to your extended family or tribe. When the majority of people are trying to make a name for themselves and feed their families, it breeds this mentality of 'me against the world.' With everybody just trying to get what they can, it makes everyone wary and skeptical. For people with the power to change things, they become reluctant to take action. They're afraid of being double-crossed by someone they thought could be trusted but to whom they never had any ties. So, they hesitate at giving any stranger a fair chance. For example, when I opened my first store in Uganda, I feared hiring people I didn't know. Having a product-based business meant it was possible for someone I was unfamiliar with to start working in my store, steal 10 dresses or more, and run off without me ever being able to track them down. With people I knew, at least I could find a way to recover the items or get payment from the families. But after hiring only people I knew, I came to realize that knowing someone didn't mean they also had the skills I needed in my store. For my business to survive, I'd need to hire the right people, regardless of whether I knew them or not. Five years later, the 'strangers' I hired are still working for me and they've all proven themselves to be great employees, fully qualified and completely loyal. But these instincts were so ingrained in me that it still took three years before I was able to hire someone I didn't know. As an employer, I was, and still am, an exception in Uganda. I don't have one simple answer as to why things are the way they are, but being aware of this as I was growing up really shaped my idea of what I could accomplish if I earned my degree but stayed. Without someone like my future self who was willing to give almost anyone a chance, there were very clearly no options for me.

I knew that if I was ever going to live the life I pictured in my mind, I would need to leave Uganda. If I could just make it to one of those places I'd seen on TV, where people had money, jobs, and things that made their lives comfortable and easy, then it shouldn't be too hard for me to save money to send back home to my family. All I needed was a chance to leave. I'd already figured out how to look for people who had money and give them something they wanted so they would share theirs with me, but there were very few people in Uganda who had money, and so it was a constant battle to get the little bit that people did have. I needed to go somewhere where there were many people with money, which would make it easier for me to make it. And the more I thought about leaving, the more I learned about places like Europe and America where people were paid by the hour. Taking into consideration the number of hours I was currently working to make approximately two hundred dollars a month, I quickly calculated what I could be making if every hour had a firm dollar value. With an opportunity like that, I could earn so much more in much less time.

At the end of the 2007 school year in December, I was left wondering what was next. I remember thinking how there was no way I could afford to go to college because, at that point, it was a significant struggle to afford the hundred dollars for tuition each term in our regular school. College would cost thousands of dollars a semester to attend, and we didn't have that kind of money. Besides, I had learned more and more about London and the U.S., including stories about people who had left Uganda and were now making immense amounts of money. I could now picture myself living in these places, working and saving my pay to buy food, clothing, and a sustainably comfortable lifestyle. I could picture my mother's face as she received the money I sent and hear my siblings' excitement when they saw the sacks of food my money bought for them. I could feel myself working at my new job during my spare time while I wasn't running my businesses. The thought of moving out of the country was a constant, waking dream in my mind. When I imagined where I could go, my pride spread through me like a warm wave. By New Year's Eve, I sat down to pray with my mom and sister, promising myself I'd leave Uganda by the end of the year.

After deciding to leave, I shared my plans with my mom and sister. I told them I was going to leave Uganda. I told my mom I was going to buy her a car. I'd said I would demolish the old house we were living in and build a brand new one in its place. I remember telling them these things with such certainty and conviction, having no doubts that this was what would happen. I could see it, I knew what I needed to do to make it happen, and I trusted myself to follow through. They kept their thoughts to themselves, saying nothing. At the time, I didn't even have a passport, so most likely, they thought I was crazy. But I had grown accustomed to being the only person who believed in me, and they had grown accustomed to showing me support through silence. And that was enough. Because as centered, balanced, and self-assured I'd become, it was still possible to hurt me in my most vulnerable places.

While I was still figuring out how to go to London, one of our neighbors, who was a low-life drunkard, had somehow learned of my plans to leave. One night, as I was going home from selling popcorn, he saw me and said in a half-drunken state, "I heard people who were supposed to go to London are still here walking barefoot." To this day, I have no idea why his words pierced me so painfully. But it conjured up every emotion and physical reaction I felt the night my aunt called me a "worthless girl." My cheeks burned hot with shame, and I felt myself shrink. This person who knew nothing about my life still felt he could disrespect it. He was mocking me, degrading me. And after all this time, accomplishing all that I had, against every obstacle and barrier in my path, I was still fighting to be seen. Still fighting to be valued, even by those who had so little value themselves. His words were a cruel question that left me shrouded in self-doubt. How much had actually changed since I was a shoeless 10-year-old girl? But through the pain, I felt the rise of anger driving me forward, and cementing my resolve. It hurt so much, but it made me want to push even harder to prove him and everyone else wrong. I was even more determined to prove myself right. A few short months later, I got my visa to go to London.

## Time To Fly

The night I got my visa, I remember laying on the floor with my sister near the bed where our mom was lying and talking about how it was so amazing that I'd made it happen. We were all so happy I don't think we slept at all. We had to keep it to ourselves despite our excitement, which left us bubbling and flushed with energy only a person hiding a fantastic secret could have. Getting a passport and visa were extremely difficult, and so both were beyond valuable. A passport and visa opened a world of opportunity in a place where none existed, and everyone was desperate for that world. We couldn't really tell anyone what was going on because we were worried someone might steal both my passport and visa, go to London pretending to be me, and leave me behind with virtually no possibility of ever getting them back.

In a few short days, I'd be flying out, but it was then my mother and sister admitted that when I told them all my plans, they did indeed think I was crazy. They told me they were, in fact, staying silent because they loved me and didn't want me to feel disappointed or discouraged. But the minute I left the house and was out of earshot, they couldn't contain themselves. "Okay, she thinks she's going to London, but she doesn't even have a passport. How is she even going to go? We don't even know anyone in outside countries. We know no one in Europe or America. How does she think she's going to any of these places?" When I walked into the house that day with both my passport and visa in my hands, they'd completely changed their minds and were ecstatic. They were thoroughly surprised, but I wasn't. I'd known all along that I would do what I'd said.

So many memories and emotions flooded my heart and mind the days leading up to my departure. Thinking about everything I'd been through, all the hurdles I had to get past, and all the days I spent working myself to death, I couldn't help but feel overwhelmed with satisfaction and relief. Every sacrifice I'd made, every shilling I'd saved, every moment I didn't give up – it had all been worth it. I was finally going to get away from the place that had tried to force an unwanted life upon me. I was finally taking concrete steps toward an imaginative future that had become so real to me. Based on what I'd learned and everything I'd been able to accomplish with what I'd been given, I was certain I would succeed. I assumed when I got to London, things would be easier. I spent my time imagining what it would be like to see the massive skyscrapers like in Dubai and New York City that I'd seen on TV, but finally in real life with my own two eyes. I thought about how I would be surrounded by White people when I got there. There were no White people where I was from. I wondered what they were like when they weren't acting in movies and TV shows. Instead of worrying about whether the area I was moving to was safe, I visualized my first plane ride as best as I could. My mind ran straight past the thought of making emergency arrangements in the event the people who were sponsoring me didn't show up to the airport to pick me up when I arrived. I then had flashes of realization that I would not have the safety of everyone I knew and understood around me. Whether the people around me actually kept me safe was one thing, but the idea of simply having them around was something that gave me comfort. I had moments when I was struck by the magnitude of leaving everything familiar and going to a place where I knew nothing, understood nothing, and would be totally and completely on my own. But looking at the visa in my hand, all the fear and uncertainty washed away. Then all I could think about was what kind of job I was going to get, what kind of investments I'd end up making, and the fact that I was finally getting to a point where I could make sure there was always food at home. I would not be "...wandering the earth like a worthless girl." I was getting out and absolutely on track toward fulfilling my dreams, and that was the only thought worth my time.

Counting all the things I've managed to do at my age, I realize how much risk I've taken on over the years, but I never looked at it that way while it was happening. I always trusted that better things awaited me on the other side. Coming of age when human trafficking ran rampant, and violence against women was a given rather than an exception, I'm beyond grateful that I've always been kept safe. Knowing what I know now, I would have definitely done my research and made sure that the place I was moving to was certainly not dangerous, but that information wasn't important to me then. Honestly, I probably wouldn't have cancelled my trip had I found out I wasn't going to be moving to a desirable town. Most likely, I would have found some way to put my mind at ease by making plans for myself and still get to work as I'd been doing for so long. Since I was 10, I had been battling through fear and uncertainty, trusting that the best way to blow through barriers is to keep on moving forward. I was an expert at succeeding by leaps of faith, and this was no exception. If I felt any fear, I felt equally strongly that the fear did not matter. The discomfort was part of this phase of moving to the next step, and once I landed and had a sense of my next move, that fear would be gone. After continuing to take the next step, and another, then the next, I would continue to do what I had always done – keep building the future I saw in my mind.

Fear can keep us frozen in inaction. It can stop us from doing so many life-changing things that if we were to let it get in the way of our dreams, we might not ever see them. But when you take a leap of faith, it's amazing what you can learn and how much you can grow as a person. Because pushing past your fears helps you to learn fairly quickly that the fear itself is not real at all, so pushing past it becomes an illusion as well. Except this illusion is so sweet, you long for it deeply. It's said that fear never leaves you, but that's not entirely true either. With fear in your mind and you in control, you can make it go away by filling your mind with other thoughts that bring you joy and excitement instead. Thoughts that can lead to amazing real-life experiences if you let them. Occupying your mind with what's pleasing to you instead of what's frightening will help you believe you have nothing to fear. This is all you'll need to conquer those things that scare everyone else. And when you do this, you instantly become unstoppable, even when it seems as if you could never make a single move. Because thinking and doing are two very different things. Only doing can take us places, but thankfully, fear resides solely in our thoughts. My pending relocation to London reminded me of all I'd done to reach that point in my life. And that taught me to never be so afraid that you don't do anything at all. Because I had done all these things, I was in the midst of becoming the adult I had always dreamt I'd be. That meant the success I craved was closer than ever before.

# PART II:
# New World View

CHAPTER 4

# Working Girl

## A lesson on accepting assurance and overcoming obstacles

### When Dreams Become Reality

On the way to London, I was so excited I couldn't even believe it was all finally happening. I'd never been on a plane before, and the thought of leaving Uganda had me filled with this immense sense of wonder and accomplishment. When I first started to seriously consider moving away, I always imagined what the ride out would be like. When it came to the plane and how it would be flying through the air, I had some very distinct thoughts. *I wonder if it has a lot of potholes like in Uganda.* I thought when you were in the air, there was no way you would hit any potholes. But on my very first flight, we had a lot of turbulence, as if the potholes were still following me. That was weird.

I remember how eager I was to try the airplane food because they gave me something I'd never eaten before. The dish was simple - some chicken, rice, broccoli, and a bun with butter. Back then, I just called it *white people food* because I had no other words to describe it. There was also a salad, but I'd never had one of those before either. I couldn't stop thinking to myself, 'Why would you give people cold leaves?' It was all so different and new to me, but mostly it was all stuff I knew I couldn't get at home, so I indulged. Once I finished eating, I felt like I'd had a five-star meal. I had left Uganda only hours before, I hadn't even reached London, and already I was eating chicken. I just sat there on the plane talking to myself, saying, "Man, this is awesome! This is what I'm going to be eating when I get there."

Before I arrived in London, the plane landed in Brussels for a very brief layover. Stepping into the airport almost sent me into sensory overload. There were crowds of people, which was not something I was unused to. People stayed close to one another in the slum where I lived in Uganda. There are crowds there just as there are in every city across the world. But what was completely foreign to me was the number of white people. In Uganda, when there is a white person around, it becomes a spectacle, especially for children. If the person is walking down the street, children will run ahead to tell others to come out and see. Throughout my childhood, I'd run to see a white person as soon as I learned where they were. As with anything rare, white people had always been intriguing to me. What they did, how they lived, what they ate, and how they were was a curious mystery. And now I was surrounded by hundreds of them. But the problem wasn't that I couldn't stop staring. It was that I couldn't possibly stare at all of them at the same time while also trying to figure out where I was going. Signs in every language everywhere, loud announcements in multiple languages, most of which I did not understand, smells of food and things in storefronts, hundreds of conversations happening as snapshots all around me – as these things flooded my senses, I was taking it in, trying to process it all at once. Walking through the airport to catch my connecting flight, there was a point where the only option to get to where I needed to go was to get on an escalator. But not the one with the stairs, the moving flat ones that are generally found at airports. I'd never seen one of them and I was so scared, but everybody was walking on it like it was normal. It was bizarre how casual they were making it all seem. The moment I stepped onto the belt, I almost fell. I looked around to see if anyone had noticed my stumble, and there were all these new faces staring right back at me.

Landing in London was just as surreal. So many days and nights I'd dreamt of this big city with bright lights and tall buildings. I couldn't believe I was finally going to be able to see it all with my own two eyes. However, driving through to where I was staying was pretty surprising. Nothing looked the way I expected. There weren't many buildings, just a lot of really old houses and extremely small roads. I also didn't see any people on the streets at all, which was odd. Nothing was like what I'd seen on TV, but it was official. I'd made it.

## Time To Get To Work

Even though I would be enrolled in a post-secondary program for graphic design and had a general interest in the subject matter, it was a means to an end. My primary reason for wanting to move to London was to get a job so I could work hourly and make money to send back home. It never occurred to me at any point that I would not be able to find a job or that I would have difficulty being hired. I was that certain. I believed there would be many jobs available, and I knew I would have one of them in no time, so I didn't waste any of it getting to my search. I touched down at 6 a.m. after what seemed like endless hours of travelling, drove to the home of my sponsor family, and immediately asked if I could use their computer. They gave me their permission, and with advice on which were the best sites to visit for job listings, they indirectly gave me their blessing. They were clearly impressed and, I thought, pleasantly surprised that my first priority was gaining employment. This was one of the first times I'd experienced what it felt like to be respected and admired for my work ethic. With their encouragement and my determination, within a couple days, I had my first job. A few short weeks later, I got a second one. I approached my job search with a level of confidence and self-assurance that must have been either shocking or refreshing for the people doing the hiring. My technique involved showing up at the address in the want ad and enthusiastically telling them I was there and ready to work. And I was successful. Finding jobs was just as easy as I had envisioned it would be. If I could do it all over again, I probably wouldn't do it that way, but it still worked out. If it was rude, then I couldn't tell by how much I was being welcomed.

With my classes in the evenings and not many of them throughout the week, I would definitely have the spare time for more than one side gig. Plus, I was used to working around the clock, and even then, I understood that no one ever became vastly wealthy off of a single source of income. I had already learned from my own small businesses that things were better and more stable when you didn't have to depend on just one way of making money. When the electricity was reliable, my candle selling business was slow, but my scrap metal sales were steady and helped to make up for it. When scrap metal was scarce, or there were fewer buyers, I had my popcorn and cake sales to back me up. I took the same approach in England. Two jobs were better than one.

With a school schedule and two jobs, I quickly fell into a routine just like I would have had I been home. Every day I would leave the house at 5 a.m. to walk the stretch of road to get to the bus stop and catch the first bus of the morning. Then the bus would drop me off near the train station. At that point, I'd get off the bus, walk the rest of the way to the train station, and catch the train to the next town over. From there, I would walk the rest of the way to the house where I worked as a caregiver and personal assistant to an elderly person. The whole commute would take approximately 45 minutes to an hour. At about 4 p.m., my client's family would come home. Once I was relieved, I'd go to my second job at a restaurant where I worked as a waitress. I'd work there until about 10 or 11 p.m., walk to the train, walk home, go to bed, wake up, and do it all over again. When I was in school, I would modify this routine, but I remained just as busy. For a while, that was my routine, and it was all I did. And I did it faithfully. I worked, I ate, I slept, then woke up to do it all over again seven days a week. And when I first arrived in the city, it was sometime in September, so just imagine how I felt doing all of this during the first winter I'd ever witnessed. I had seen snow on TV, and conceptually, I knew what it was. But I soon learned it was far more appealing and fun on TV than in reality. The average temperature in Kampala is 80ºF, and the coldest it gets is around 65ºF. I had felt cold, but never stinging, painful cold. I had been wet many times at home, but never the kind of post-freezing wet that burns. Walking one mile in pleasant weather felt like five in the biting wind and drifts of snow. Regardless, I still did what I had to do every single day, even if that meant facing temporary pain and discomfort.

With time, things began paying off, and before I knew it, I was sending a check home that was worth 1,000 pounds. At Western Union, I could barely hold back my excitement as I filled out the paperwork for the transfer. The exchange rate for the check ended up being something like 4.5 million Ugandan shillings. That was an insane amount of money to me. And I had made it all in about two weeks time. The fact that in just two weeks, I'd made an amount of money that would've probably taken me about a year to make back home was so mind-boggling. I told my sister, "Go get a hundred-pound bag of rice, make sure you get a hundred-pound bag of beans…" Basically, the entire amount was spent on food, but that's exactly what I wanted. If we could stock up on food, then we could avoid the way we'd been living before I left. That was the most important thing. There was also a bit of pride. I thought about how things had been for me growing up. From my aunt saying those things about us to my mom going through everything she had to go through as a widow with two little girls in tow. I thought about my aunt's scowling face as she spat out the words *worthless girl*, the drunken neighbor mocking my bare feet, the girls taunting one of my two dresses, and the tiny smiles that always flicked over the school administrators' faces when they sent me to clean toilets. But instead of feeling anger or shame, I felt thrilled. They had bet against me and lost.

I couldn't stop thinking about the neighbors and how they'd talk. Everyone in my neighborhood was always in everyone else's business, and gossip was the norm. They would know immediately that I was sending extravagant amounts of money home, and I knew what they would say. They'd say the same things about me that they'd said about the family that lived down the street from us, the one with the daughter that lived out of the country. Whenever she would send them food and whatever other new things we could spot, we'd all be talking about it for the entire day. Everyone. I kept envisioning my sister going and buying all this food and all the neighbors seeing it. I knew exactly what comments would come up the moment they saw. *Ah? Did you see they got some food? Oh my God. How lucky they are.* The word would spread to the people who had doubted and diminished me. As I stood in that Western Union office, it finally felt like my life had reached a turning point. I had changed my circumstances and was now in a position to truly improve the circumstances for the people I loved. This money and my status did more than provide food. Everyone used to call us losers and talk about us like we were useless, but at that point, I felt like we were becoming one of the more respected families, and that felt amazing.

Because I was enrolled in school, I had to show up to my classes and do my work. But my mind and my priorities were often in other places. I decided on graphic design as I applied and chose my course work mostly because I had always had an interest in it. But it also turned out to have some of the cheaper courses you could take, and that was definitely an added benefit. I'd also found out the curriculum would give me greater flexibility in my class schedule, which was honestly what I wanted the most so I'd be able to work more. Before long, my reputation as a compassionate, reliable, and accomplished caregiver spread. I was offered a second position with another family, adding a third job to my already packed schedule. As much as I enjoyed graphic design as a craft, this left me with little time to perfect the skills I was supposed to be learning. I would go to class, but I would always be rushing in from one job to leave in a rush to get to the other. The truth was, I never saw myself as a career graphic designer. My focus was entrepreneurship, and I knew that I was born to be a business owner. Still, I gave the effort to my coursework, which turned out to be a good thing. It was from a graphic design project that my next business venture sparked.

I had learned that people in Europe would often visit African countries for vacationing, mostly places like Egypt, or to others for safaris and sightseeing. For one of my graphic design projects, I developed a website for a safari travel booking business, then began offering safari vacation services. I knew people in Africa, knew where the travel spots were, and knew enough to help potential vacationers and safari enthusiasts plan their trips. That is how, in my spare time around school and three jobs, I began operating a small, online travel agency, booking safaris in Uganda for eager vacationers. Things had changed. I had moved worlds away and was having all these new experiences. But I was still very much a dreamer and creating opportunities for myself and others.

The two families I was working with loved me and appreciated the work I was doing with their elders so much, they began talking about me to their friends and acquaintances. I had gotten the second caregiving job through my first family's referral, and now there were more and more families contacting me and asking if I could help. By then, I'd met a couple of girls who were also looking for work and who I thought might make a good fit for the jobs. They were also African and we were all going to the same school, so I approached each of them and said flat out, "If you want to make some extra pounds, I can get you a job." Within three weeks, these girls were working for me. Handling any and all communication with the families, I would send each girl to whatever house I knew needed help. For services, families would be charged 20 pounds per hour, and depending on their skills, abilities, and performance, each of the girls would earn 15 to 17 pounds per hour. Making sure I was rightfully compensated for all the work I was doing, I'd charge the families directly, collect from them, then pay the girls after subtracting my own administrative fees of 3 to 5 pounds per hour. Between my budding safari travel agency, my home care company, and the hours I worked directly as a caregiver and waitress, I was earning quite a bit of money. I continued to send money home, as well as save as much as I could. Because of my status as a student and the precarious nature of my visa, I was worried it could all suddenly end.

## Every Detour Leads To A New Path

When you have a Ugandan passport, you need some kind of visa to go virtually anywhere at any given time. For me to go to London, I applied for a visitor visa, but I knew from the very beginning it was only going to be valid for six months. My plan was to apply for a student visa before my visitor visa expired and stay for as long as possible until I figured out my next steps. But close to the end of my three months in the UK, my application for my new visa was denied.

I couldn't believe it. I hardly had any time to adjust to my new lifestyle or really appreciate my new surroundings, and now I was faced with this big decision. Either I'd stay in the country illegally and continue working or go back home to Uganda and try my hardest to get back. As much as I wanted to stay, it felt like I really didn't have any choice. The whole point of me traveling to another country was to eventually start and own my own business, but I couldn't do that there if I stayed after my visa expired. I was so disappointed. After all that planning, all that hoping and dreaming that life would be better, and all I had was three measly months to spread my wings. I knew I had to leave London, but I wasn't ready to go back home.

Before finding out the news, I had a feeling it would be difficult to get the student visa, so I'd already spent some time thinking about a plan B. I had the idea for the safari business, but after vacationing in Egypt with one of the families I was working for, I realized how easy it would be to get a good-paying job at a resort town there. With that, my mind was made. I would drop out of school, take the four or five-hour flight from London to Egypt, and start all over there. A few days before I was scheduled to leave, I had a dream about my dad. Before that, I had never really dreamt about him. I think maybe there was one time before, but nothing significant that I can remember. But in this dream, my dad came to me and spoke directly to my heart. In his own way he let me know things were going to be hard, but everything was okay. I would be okay. In the days leading up to my departure, that was one of the only things I thought about. I'd been faced with this massive bump in the road, but I was sure it wasn't the end of my journey. There were still more side hustles for me to start and more businesses to brainstorm. I still had the chance to become the kind of caring person for my family that my father was. I just needed some time to regroup.

## Finding Opportunities In Obstacles

It's funny how easily our plans can be derailed. We have this idea of exactly how we believe things will go because we're so experienced in making plans and having them work out. But in reality, everything doesn't always end that way. No matter how badly they hurt to maneuver, sometimes detours are necessary. Truthfully, it's those few extra stops on our journey that can make the trip that much more fulfilling. Of course, this isn't the feeling we automatically think of when faced with trying times. However, it's only after we've gone through our worst moments that we recognize how we needed them to grow into our best selves. The bright side of it all was, if I left school, then I could start making money the way I wanted. Crunching the numbers, I realized that if I just took my time and went to work, I'd easily be making a lot more money than if I were to find a way to finish school. I took courses in graphic design, but I was also taking courses in business administration and I was learning a lot. Thinking critically, I said to myself, "Okay. If I finish school, get my degree, and get a job, I'll be making about 50,000 pounds a year on average, starting out at maybe 40,000 pounds a year." That might have been enough for some people, but with all the responsibilities I had with my family back home and how I was taking care of everyone now, it was obvious that amount was never going to be enough for me.

Failure is virtually unavoidable, especially when our plans are so big. I wasn't completely sure if I was making the right decision, but there was ultimately no way for me to know the answer until I tried and waited to see what the outcome would be. In hindsight, what I had been able to do in the little bit of time I was in London was an accomplishment in and of itself, but the immature part of me wasn't fully pleased with my stay. I kept feeling like I could have done more. More studying during school hours or more work during the week or more side hustling in my spare time. Then maybe it all would've added up to more money or opportunities for me to flip. But once I sat down and really gave it some thought, I realized I had actually done quite a lot considering my status as a young woman coming from a completely different continent. Leaning on all the things I'd learned about life and business up until that point, I excelled in this brand new place I knew very little about, and that was something I could be happy with. I made sure to prioritize my time outside of school just as I'd done all the years I was growing up, and it paid off tremendously. I embraced the things I knew better than anyone else and became a highly sought-after caregiver, travel consultant, and employment agent, all in one. Equally uplifting was realizing that I could go into a different culture with a different language, customs, and expectations and still find ways to create lucrative opportunities for myself. I simply treated the place I was living like it was my home and found ways to improve it just as I would've done in Uganda. I identified problems that needed solving, and I solved them in creative ways. And maybe I wasn't the only one around who knew how to solve these problems, but I was surely the only one around doing anything about them.

Every moment we're working toward our dreams, we are inevitably risking defeat. But whenever we reach obstacles that make the road that much more difficult to traverse, that's when our true selves are fully revealed. Before I left Uganda, everything I'd put my mind to had worked out. Sometimes even better than I anticipated. Facing this new situation in London, I saw the woman I was quickly shaping up to be. When things hadn't fully gone my way, of course I was upset, but I didn't give up. Instead, I used the rest of my energy to figure out how to recover. I used my time and attention to pivot into a better situation. Because obstacles are always going to come along, whether we've dealt with them before or not is irrelevant. It's how we approach these problems that reveals our true intentions, strengths, and every so often, our weaknesses.

Failure is an unmistakable stepping stone toward success, but only if we look at it as a stone to step on and not a boulder blocking the way. The moment I decided to relocate to Egypt instead of going back to Uganda, I proved to myself I wouldn't stop chasing the goals I initially set out to achieve. It showed me how much of an entrepreneur I was, finding ways to make extra money when my jobs weren't paying enough and forgoing formal schooling for the chance to create something that could sustain my family for years to come. That one decision to try something new once my visa application was denied let me know that behind every obstacle is a better opportunity. We just have to be open and willing to notice it when it comes.

For many years I thought very little about my experience in London. I'd been there for such a short time I rarely thought about it, let alone considered it something worth mentioning. One of my purposes of going to London was to attend school, which I did not finish, and for the longest, I passed it off as a sideline in my life story. It was like the transition gate between Uganda and everything that came after it. But the more I thought about my stay in London, the more I understood just how pivotal my experiences were to everything that followed. I came to appreciate everything I'd learned, and I'd seen all I was capable of. I noticed how easy it was to start a side hustle wherever I went, even if I was unfamiliar with the area or the people. By complementing my lifestyle with the skills I already had and the things I already knew, I was able to smoothly operate several enterprises and create multiple streams of income from very little. I noticed how good I was at not only making money, but setting the goals I needed to save and invest. It felt so amazing to be able to help out back home with everything I set aside. I knew now that I had started, I was never going to stop providing like that. And most of all, I accepted that school just wasn't for me. As a child, I wanted to grow up, become a lawyer, and get a great job. My father had been educated in the States, and I wanted to follow his prestigious path. But the business theories and marketing techniques I was learning about in class were things I was doing in reality. I learned how to scale my one-person enterprises into a mini-company in a very short amount of time. When

I had to leave my little home care operation behind, I had four employees servicing several different clients. For the first time, I finally understood a way to add more hours to the day. The key was to bring on more people so it was possible to do more work. It was so natural and easy to make this transition. It made me realize that while there was a limit on my time, there was no limit to the amount of work I could create by adding people to my team.

While studying graphic design, I'd also learned what became the basis of my business development process - take inventory of what you have, figure out what you can do, and understand what it is that other people need. I found putting those things together in such a way created money without needing money. In addition to these business basics, I learned about the importance of quality, customer service, and networking. My outstanding work led people to refer me to others, which led me to more work. I attribute the fact that I have built multiple international enterprises from the confidence I developed during my short time in London. But most importantly, my time in the UK was the foundation of my development as an entrepreneur. Taking note of my achievements helped me trust and believe that I knew what I was doing. I was pleased to recognize I didn't need a certificate to spell it out.

Whenever you're trying to accomplish anything, there will be so many times when you feel like it's time to give up. There will be so many instances where you believe all the signs point to stopping. But you must leave any excuses you encounter right where you found them. Facing three months of the first and worst winter of my life would have been an easy excuse for me not to work as hard as I did outside of my classes, but I didn't let it influence me.

If I'd accepted the denial of my visa application as the end, then I might have never ended up in Egypt to do and see all of the things and places I have today. I refused to quit when it would have been acceptable for anyone else to do so. The truth is, obstacles can temporarily detour us, but until we decide to stop altogether, our journeys will always continue. It's only ourselves who can get in the way of reaching what we want, not the things in the outside world that seem to slow us down. By the time I was ready to relocate to Egypt, I'd decided that nothing I encountered could ever stop me from achieving my dreams. No matter how glaring the problem, I knew that I would always figure out a way to get through because I was dead set on moving forward. That way, whenever I was faced with any roadblocks or forks in the road, I didn't hesitate. I always knew exactly what would happen next.

In London, I hit my very first big and real obstacle. Having to think, problem solve, and pivot in a new direction gave me a new outlook on fear and the potential for failure. I acquired a problem-embracing mindset that I now use to create opportunities. If you begin thinking about, focusing on, and worrying about problems, barriers, and risks, that will be all you see and encounter as you move forward. Where the mind goes, actions follow. And what you focus on is where you will end up. Instead of stamping the experience as a failure, I embraced the situation as a problem to be solved, a challenge to overcome, or a barrier to remove. Instead of seeing my application denial as the end, I saw it as a signal to pivot and do something – anything, in fact – to not wind up back in Uganda where I'd started. I knew any move I made would gain ground.

In life and business, I have learned to assume both barriers and opportunities will always come. And when they do, they arrive hand in hand. Whenever an obstacle arrives, problem-solving solutions, which are inevitably the next opportunities, quickly reveal themselves. I realized that even by trying and utterly failing, you find yourself in no better or worse a position than where you initially stood. But if the barrier still exists, then the solution is not far behind. You just have to give it time. Layovers happen on flights and in life, but if we don't recognize them for what they are, we might get stuck in all the wrong places. The same goes for detours. Your journey may take a bit longer to complete, but it never ends where the road seems to. For so long, I thought London was where I was going to end up. But the big city where I'd spent so little time turned out to be where I got my start as an international entrepreneur and the springboard for the rest of my life.

# CHAPTER 5

# A New World

## A lesson on being receptive to new experiences

By the time my plane from London touched down in Egypt, I had resolved any lingering feelings of disappointment and was truly looking forward to whatever would come next. From the brief time I'd spent in Egypt on vacation with my caregiving clients, I knew the vacation and tourism industry there was healthy. From my experience working in London, I'd developed a sense of what types of jobs would keep me moving forward. Jobs that required more than just my labor would pay better and give me more potential for growth in my own businesses. I'll admit, I would have taken a job serving tables, cleaning, or working in any position I could get to support myself. But I knew I wanted more than just an hour-to-hour hustle. I wanted to use my brain, and give myself the opportunity to gain invaluable transferable skills. Pretty quickly, I landed a position in guest relations in the prestigious resort town of Hurghada, located on the Red Sea coast.

## Meeting People Where They Were

Hurghada is one of the main tourist centers in its part of the country, and it was always bustling. Drawing in countless visitors from around the world eager to enjoy their holidays, it was a prime location for vacationing and working. Mostly because there was no real off-season. The weather was regularly dry, and the 25 miles of beautiful beaches were calm year-round. This meant there was always a need for help to take care of tourists. No lapse in tourism meant a steady stream of customers for me, making Hurghada the perfect place to settle down and carve out a new niche for myself. Even settling in felt easy. Living and working on the resort was the perfect way for me to bounce back from what had happened with my visa in London, mostly because it didn't always feel like work. It was just so beautiful on the resort, almost like paradise. I was surrounded by people who were there to relax and enjoy themselves, and I was making such great money it sometimes felt more like a surreal vacation than anything else. That's not to say everything was perfect because anyone with a job will tell you that being an employee is anything but. There were definitely moments that kept me firmly attached to reality. For example, have you ever spoken to someone in guest relations during your expensive vacation at an international resort? Most likely if you have, then you were complaining. Dealing with customer complaints wasn't my favorite aspect of the job, but it did give me yet another set of skills that have been invaluable to me in the years that followed.

Customers are not swayed by facts they've overlooked, and they will never change their perception even if you point out the obvious. A vacationer who believes a room upgrade will be given believes they deserve one. Even if you point out in their confirmation where it plainly states the room assigned is the one they booked. Customers want what they expect, and if they don't get what they pictured, there's usually a problem. More often than not, I'd have to bend reality to avoid those kinds of problems. From other unhappy customers' experiences, I also learned how to listen patiently and carefully, gain valuable perspective, and meet people where they were. A person complaining because the water in their room is too cold will not stop and feel better if I tell them how lucky they are that their bed is not on the floor. Or that they aren't routinely covered with muddy flood water at 2 am like I was growing up. No matter what other issues they could possibly be facing, their cold water situation is real and important to them now. No matter how trivial, small, or insignificant the complaint or concern, people just want to be sure that you've acknowledged them, even if there's not much you can do. Sometimes, they simply want to unload and get sympathy. Often after they've aired everything out, their problems feel resolved. Other times, they would tell me exactly what they wanted, and I could solve the problem then and there. I learned to ask plenty of questions, drawing out what customers needed to effectively resolve their issues. Most importantly, I learned to keep my reactions and facial expressions neutral when someone was demanding, obnoxious, or unreasonable. All of these skills have been beyond valuable to me as an entrepreneur. Whether I am buying properties, negotiating multimillion-dollar deals, engaging with employees, or developing my next business endeavor, I draw on the skills I learned standing behind that customer service desk in Egypt.

 Small annoyances aside, I loved my job. I appreciated the work for what it was and also what it brought me – steady pay that I could use to map out my goals for moving forward. With the money I earned, I had a safe place to live, food to eat every day, and enough savings to invest in my future business endeavors. My job also gave me access to clients for a special boat cruise I'd organized. There were small islands in the middle of the Red Sea, and I made connections with people who owned small yachts. I would set romantic picnics for couples at these islands, and get them a boat to take them there with drinks and snacks for 2-4 hours. It was an added luxury many of the vacationers appreciated to have at their disposal. As something not advertised beforehand, tourists often jumped at the unexpected opportunity to enhance their stay at the resort. After paying for the boat and refreshments, I would profit $100 to $200 per trip. Scheduling two trips a day on average, I was doing very well for myself.

In no time at all, I was thriving, almost as if I'd planned to leave London the entire time. However, in the back of my mind, it was still my plan to return to the UK. It was where I was drawn to. It was in a place like London or somewhere in the US where the playing field seemed more even. I was eager to establish myself someplace where real, life-changing opportunities were open to me. As I worked and lived in Egypt, I treated the experience as a transition. I decided all I would have to do was be productive and patient until my visa was granted, then I'd be on the next flight back. Funny how easily the best-laid plans can change.

## Making Room For Something New

When you fall in love, it's almost like you have no say in the matter. Some people can tell you the exact moment in time when they fell in love. They saw the person from across the room, their eyes locked, they felt swept away, and from that moment on, they were fully and deeply connected. Other people don't have that experience. For others, it's a slow build of affection over time, where a hundred little looks and moments and experiences pile up and collect around you like grains of sand until suddenly, you look around yourself and realize you're standing on a beach. All these little things that you like about a person just pile up until you realize something profound. Slowly, but seemingly all at once, you come to notice you don't want to live the way you used to, without experiencing all of those little things. And that's the way it was for me. There isn't an actual day or moment I can look back on and say that was when I fell in love. But I do remember the moments when I felt the man I'd met was special, and the feelings I felt for him were different. Missing him when he was away, feeling happier when I was with him, getting a little rush when I heard his voice, and finally realizing at one point that I did not want to picture my life without him in it. These were events I'd never expected, but when they arrived, I didn't hesitate to let them in.

When I met my husband, I didn't necessarily think he would later become my husband. As he walked up to the desk where I was working, there certainly was no lightning strike moment. I just remember thinking he was very good looking, but nothing more than my next customer. However, we connected. His sense of humor was the thing that roped me into dating him. He'd just moved to Cairo for his job, which was about an hour flight away from where I was in Hurghada, and he was staying at our resort. I'd seen him from time to time, just as I saw the other resort guests in passing, but I never thought much of it. Then one day, he came to my desk and began talking to me. We spoke for a little while, and it was almost like he was trying to complain about something, but I wasn't entirely sure what was going on at first. Being the fantastic customer service professional I was, I listened politely, patiently absorbing his complaint, and enthusiastically ready to do what I could to make this handsome customer's stay at the resort even better. But the more he said, the more difficult I found it to figure out what his complaint actually was. He was being very vague, and it did not occur to me for a moment that he was joking. Now I know this is something he does all the time when he wants to be cheeky. He complains about something without having any real thing to complain about. But before I knew him and how he joked, it was just confusing to me. There he was making up odd complaints that weren't actual complaints, and there I was trying to get to the bottom of the issue and solve the problem. I was utterly clueless to the fact that he was flirting, and that made him even more amused by me. When I finally realized he wasn't actually complaining, he pretended to be hurt (just another way for him to be cheeky). In a way, it made me feel bad. I guess it read across my face because almost immediately, he said, "Oh, it's alright. You can make it up by going to dinner with me." I felt the answer leap out of my mouth. "Okay." *Why not see where this goes?*

After our first date, we couldn't stop texting each other. My husband used to travel a lot for his job, but we made sure to make time for each other when we started dating. He would make every opportunity we could spend together his first and highest priority, and I could tell how important I was to him. To this day, I still wonder how he did it. After we met, it was like his rest took a back seat to our relationship. To understand how significant this is, you need to know something about my husband – he is a sleeper. A really good one. Absolutely nothing gets between him and a few hours of sleep. It is beyond a priority and nearly a passion for him. But after we met, every spare moment, including those precious potential sleeping hours, belonged to me. Honestly, I wasn't sleeping much either. If I wasn't working, sleeping, thinking about him, or working while thinking about him, we were talking. He traveled to Europe quite often, and if he landed after a full day of work at 11 p.m., then by midnight, he'd be in his hotel talking to me on the phone. Even though we both had to get up early for work in the morning, it didn't matter to either of us. 1 a.m., 2 a.m., 3 a.m.... we couldn't stop talking. We just couldn't hang up. It felt impossible to break the connection, and once we did, I would lay awake thinking about my future husband until it was time to get up. For six straight months, beginning the night of our first date, we talked every night on the phone. And every single night, it was the same. If I was in Hurghada and he was in Cairo, Europe or wherever, we talked until the time came when we finally agreed to stop. There's no telling how much sleep we would have missed out on had we not forced ourselves to hang up. Soon, we were visiting each other most weekends, and parting with him at the end of each one became harder and harder. Now I was spending each night talking to him and each day looking forward to seeing him. I didn't think about it then, but I was falling fast in love.

While my husband and I were dating, I'd been working alongside another young woman whose boyfriend had recently proposed to her. Like most future brides, she was swept up in the excitement of an upcoming wedding and frequently spoke about her plans. Each day she described the type of dress she would wear, how many guests she would invite, the food, the ceremony, and other details every bride obsesses over as they plan their day. She had been thinking about and planning her wedding since she was a child. She was so excited to bring this dream to life. I realized I hadn't thought about getting married or what my own wedding day would be like since I was a child before my dad died. Once he was gone, dreams like that went with him. Before my dad's death, the most I imagined about my adult life was becoming a lawyer, having a big white wedding, having kids, and living happily ever after. But by then, everything about my life was dramatically different. I had grown to be a realist. I wasn't that same little girl anymore, and I knew I didn't want the same things. I couldn't see myself trying to create a fantasy wedding day.

In Uganda, every wedding is *huge*. When you have a wedding there you rarely ever see a ceremony as small as 50 people. There are no intimate gatherings of your closest friends and family. There are also no guest lists, invitations, or cut-offs when it comes to attendees. It is a given that the whole family is invited. And recall, please, the word family is expansive and includes everyone who is even loosely attached to a related person. Your father's first wife's nephew's daughter would count as family, just as your half-sister's husband's brother would. Aunties, uncles, first, second, and third cousins are all family. They are all coming to your wedding. There are no worries about leaving someone off the guest list or forgetting to extend an invitation to anyone. All of the neighbors will be in attendance as well. If they live in the general vicinity, hear about the wedding, or even suspect it may be happening, they will be there. The entire town knows, and everyone shows up. Even if there are people you aren't expecting to attend, they might be walking by, see there's a wedding going on, stop, grab some food, talk for a little bit, and maybe get in a dance or two.

I had grown up in a culture where weddings were a time of great togetherness and celebration, but the thought no longer appealed to me. A major part of the wedding is the extended family, namely the bride's father's family. Whomever I married would have to pay a dowry to my aunties and uncles, the very people in my extended family who I did not care for at all. People who had thrown my mother, sister, and I out of our home and our livelihood, then turned their backs on us for years, allowing us to struggle to survive. None of those people in my family had helped us or given us any kind of support while we were growing up, so the thought of giving them money made me furious. At that point, I no longer considered them family, but that wouldn't stop them from expecting the tradition to be followed. As far as my neighborhood was concerned, there was so much gossip and backbiting in the area. Those people had been so cruel and demeaning to my mother, sister and me that they would not be coming to my wedding out of love or support. They would be coming to find new ways of being insulting. There was no way I'd ever want any of those people to show up to my wedding just so they could tear me down to feel better about themselves.

A huge Ugandan wedding was the last thing I wanted. After all my years of working, striving, and struggling to earn my money, there would be no way I would spend it on people I didn't like. I had no interest in feeding them, buying them drinks, or treating them to thank-you gifts. In my opinion, they deserved none of it. But a part of me began to think that if I did get married, how amazing it would be to be married to him. I quickly began fantasizing about our small civil ceremony with my mom, my sisters, and maybe a couple of friends with us to share the moment. That way I wouldn't have to waste $20k on a big white wedding I was no longer interested in hosting. With that much money I felt like I could put a down payment on a house and be way better off. I wasn't sure if he had a big family, but I figured we could fill in the rest of the guest list with them if they were interested in attending. I had been so detached from the idea of marriage for so long. But for some reason, it did not seem strange to me that I was suddenly creating a guest list in my mind, thinking of locations for the ceremony, and imagining myself marrying this man whom I'd only recently met a few months prior. Things were moving fast, but I felt everything he'd shown me up to that point was all I needed to know. With him, I'd have someone interested in spending time with me, even routinely sacrificing their sleep to hear me recite all my plans for the future. Knowing I had someone who would spend hours listening to my dreams and ambitions, supporting and encouraging everyone, filled me with joy. Recognizing I could share all my innermost thoughts and emotions in great detail without fear or reservation felt overwhelmingly freeing. And when he surprised my sister (and me) with a stroller for her baby, I knew for sure I wanted him to be my husband. Any fear I might've had about taking care of my family went away because I knew he understood how much they meant to me. He wasn't going to keep me from seeing them or helping them with bills, food, or whatever else they needed. And with that one small gift, he made them his family too. I was in love. I trusted he would continue to be the same gentle person I met in Hurghada, and at that point, I was sold on the idea of getting married. We'd met near the end of 2008. By October 2009, we were engaged.

By the time I'd met my husband, I'd learned that men will be men wherever you go. But for a large part of my life, I held this skewed idea of marriage and romantic relationships. This may sound bad, but after knowing how my dad lived and understanding how his romantic habits affected his life and the lives of his children, it always made me feel like I never wanted to marry an African man. I genuinely believed that if my dad had not married that maid woman, he probably would've lived a few years longer. Part of what attracted me to my future husband was that he wasn't African. I had this belief that Western men were different. They didn't need to marry multiple women because they loved and could be fully devoted to the one they had. I'd believed it wasn't as much in the nature of Western men to mistreat their wives as freely or as badly as the men around me growing up did. Unfortunately, I had been unlucky to grow up without the example and influence of good, loving, and supporting men around, so what became attractive to me was decidedly non-African. Something in me felt that falling in love with an African man would eventually lead me to betrayal and misery. My mother had been through so much in her own marriages, and so had a couple of my sisters. Every once in a while, they would come home with their faces bloodied and bruised because their husbands had beat them up for whatever worthless reasons. From the ones who were supposed to love them, they had no recourse or possibility of protection. I just wanted a man who was nothing like these men I'd grown up around. Since I couldn't be 100% sure my husband wouldn't be like that, I had no choice but to trust my gut.

Meeting my husband was probably the best lesson I could've ever had in leaning on my own intuition. Following the path that led me to fall in love with him was not something I had planned. In fact, it was nowhere on my mind or anything I could have envisioned happening. I wasn't looking for a man to take care of my family or me, I was just doing what I had always planned to do. I was focused on working and saving as much as I could to cover the investments I was building. My vision for my future self was to be the provider my family needed, and it did not include someone else as a partner. I hadn't thought about marriage or kids since I was a little girl when my life had been drastically different, yet everything inside me was saying this was the right thing to do. Suddenly, just by meeting this person, my vision shifted. Now there was someone I trusted, someone I could rely on. Someone to be my partner in everything to come. All the times he'd shown me the kind of man he was, I believed him. And I genuinely liked him, so I wasn't afraid of letting my guard down. I was just excited to get to know him. When we were engaged, I stopped working in Hurghada and moved to where he was living in Cairo. Before I met my husband, I had every intention of returning to London as soon as possible to get back to business. But after I fell for him, that plan no longer served me. I moved in with him right away to get started on living our lives together, and I could get back to focusing on my goals. I was assured that my voice would always be heard, so it didn't feel like I was giving up anything. I would have a stable household to live in, more free time to devote to my enterprises, and companionship with someone I loved very much and whom I knew felt the same way about me. Even though the thought of marriage had put a sour taste in my mouth at one time, that didn't mean this relationship would be that way.

Up until that point, I alone had created every opportunity I pursued. I pictured what I wanted and carefully chose meaningful steps to get there. I did not believe in things like opportunities falling into my lap because that was not how my life worked. If I wanted or needed something, I had to create the opportunities that set me on the path. But this was totally different. I did not seek my husband out, and I was not looking for him. But here he was. It was the first time I realized the value of my own instincts. I finally understood the wisdom in recognizing when a wonderful but unexpected opportunity falls in your lap and the importance of fighting back logic and fear to seize that opportunity. As an entrepreneur, most of the opportunities I pursue are ones that I've created myself. My healthcare company and retail businesses were results of months of research, time, determination and effort. They were all opportunities I had to thoughtfully create and execute largely on my own. But after meeting my husband and taking the leap of faith, I learned to look for opportunities that were waiting for someone to scoop them up and make them into something incredible. My water filter company started with an idea I carried in my mind for years, until the opportunity to bring it to life arose. My Entrepreneurship for Women enterprise had a similar beginning. The opportunity presented itself and my actions followed. Learning to see opportunity as something that can be created and given has been invaluable. Taking the leap of faith to marry my husband was the very experience that helped me to understand that.

## Finding A Way To Maintain Independence

I never really had a real friend until secondary school. I changed schools so much my friendships just couldn't last. I did make a good friend in high school, but after two months of knowing them, I had to change schools again. We did eventually reunite, but we'd lost touch for about five years. Before that, I mostly spent my time with all the other kids in my neighborhood. We were all in similar situations, most of them worse off than I was. But we were always hungry. That's where we bonded. Technically, these kids weren't my friends. Really I'd only spend time with them during the holidays when there was no school and more time in my day. They were my team. We would go hunting together for food, working in numbers to make it easier for us to succeed. We were undeniably independent, but we operated with each other in mind. That kind of relationship was very similar to what I was looking for in my marriage. When I got married, we wouldn't necessarily have to be with each other every moment of the day. We would be two separate people often coming together as one to reach a common goal. We would be working to build a better life as partners compared to anything we could have created on our own.

In Cairo, my transition from life as a single woman to one in a committed relationship went very smoothly. Mostly, I believe it was because we continued to see one another as independent people who were now part of our own little personal team. We trusted the idea that two people could be together in a state of equality, where both person's needs were important without one being greater than the other's. We would have our own personal goals and our common goals. But most importantly, what we could do together would be much more significant than what we could accomplish individually. Now that I have had the opportunity to meet, speak to, and coach other women in business, I am beginning to understand how different my experience in marriage has been from so many others. Being married to a fellow career and work-focused person means we understand one another's drive, ambition, and commitment to professional success. It also makes us both fiercely independent individuals who shift to strike a comfortable balance between our personal and professional worlds. At times, it becomes a struggle. But what I have been careful to do is prevent it from becoming an obstacle. Many of the women I coach on entrepreneurship list their husbands and families as barriers to their success. They have less time because they have to respond and cater to the needs of their families, or they can't see themselves moving forward because they do not have the faith, support, or encouragement of their husbands.

Marriage is not designed to kill our dreams or squash our ambitions, so if you have a lot of those, or even just one, you should never lose yourself or let go of what you want just to appease your partner's wishes. Strangely enough for women, it feels like something we are supposed to accept as par for the course. Marriage should be a genuine union involving two independent people that choose to walk this journey of life together. It should be a meeting of two people who collaborate to bring forth solutions that work in the best interest of both parties. But more often than not, needs are viewed as mutually exclusive. *These are mine, those are yours.* But when this is the case, any compromise is always seen as *who wins and who loses.* Generally, the expectation is for the mom, the wife, the woman to stand down. Inevitably, she ends up losing most of the time. My advice for those women unsure of whether they should enter a marriage while working toward their goals is this: whatever you do, make sure that it makes *you* happy. Because as long as you're happy, you will have built the foundation for a happy marriage. Many of the women I coach have become so focused on everyone else's happiness, that they set their own aside along with their hopes and dreams. They see happiness as a hierarchy. They put their drive and desire for success at the bottom of the list, thinking happiness for everyone at the same time just isn't possible. Many started out ambitious, focused and driven, but over time, took hundreds of small steps that put the needs of others over their own, until it became a habit. Unfortunately, it's a way of life that began because of best intentions. But what that produces is the opposite of happiness for everyone. Marriage is a committed partnership. It's a unique union where you share everything, from responsibilities to riches. If you're choosing to make someone your partner, you can never compromise on your happiness. Making sure you can be happy by yourself is important before entering any serious relationship because there is no one else in this world besides you that can make you consistently feel that way. If you leave your happiness up to outside factors, even up to those you love, you're giving them an easy chance to fall short of what you could ultimately offer yourself. This can lead to dependency issues that create the perfect environment for things to fall apart.

It's funny, whenever my husband talks about our first date, without fail, he describes it as a high stress interrogation! *Did you go to college? Have you been married before? Do you have any kids from any previous relationships?* There were no questions or conversations that I thought were too personal for a person I'd just met. The biggest thing I learned from my dad's passing was how much my mom truly depended on him. My mother is a very smart woman and a hard worker, but once he was gone, and she was left with next to nothing, the contrast between what my father brought to the table while they were married and what she had brought was clearly visible. My mother was capable of caring for herself and everyone around her in the time leading up to her marriage to my father, but I can only imagine that while they were together, she became relaxed and complacent. She'd started to depend on him rather than herself. By the time I met my husband, I had substantial responsibilities in Uganda. I'd been so consistent over the years with my businesses that I was now helping to support my mom, my half-sisters, nieces and nephews. My family relied heavily on me for many things and would need me to continue supporting them even after I was married. I wasn't trying to do anything that could jeopardize that. But when I thought about everything the both of us brought to the table, I became less worried. I had the confidence that comes with finding multiple ways to earn money as a child, on top of finding work to support myself in not one, but two foreign countries in less than two years. There was no doubt in my mind that opportunities would always be there for me, regardless of whether I needed to create them myself or search until I found them. Then there was my future husband, who had an advanced education and a six-figure salary to show for it. He was born, raised, and educated in the US, which, even if we never decided to live there, provided a source of stability and security for us and our future family together. And I hated school. With the very slim chance of me ever going back, I figured if at least one of us had a degree, it would count for something if we were to have kids together. And more importantly, any children we did have would be firsts for us both. Neither of us had been married before or had children from previous relationships. Growing up, I had so many half-siblings, it was difficult to feel like I had a special or exclusive attachment. My strongest bond was with the only sister I shared both of my parents with. We were close in age, spent all of our time together, and shared a connection we didn't have with any of our parents' other kids. I wanted that same feeling of connection, belonging, and attachment for my children. Plus, I would be the only mother in our children's lives. There would be no other wives or husbands to tolerate or endure, or loosely affiliated immediate family relationships that we'd have to navigate. Considering all these things, I stood to gain so much in marrying my husband. I was confident marriage would be a far different experience for me than it had been for my mother.

Still, my eyes remained open to the possibility that everything could change in a heartbeat. Yes, I loved him. I wanted to marry him. I wanted to be with him for as long as we both would live, but I wasn't naive to the fact that life happens and neither of us would live forever. Things change, and I was no stranger to the concept. *What if I suddenly lose my husband the way I lost my father? What if everything we have is instantly lost? What if some tragedy or circumstance we cannot control breaks us? How will either one of us be secure if something happens to the other?* I didn't think it was likely, but he could even wake up any day and decide he wanted to be with someone else. Then what would I have? Although I trusted my husband and believed I would always be supported and taken care of by him, the answer was clear to me – I would need to continue working and earning my own money.

To me, marriage wasn't some sort of achievement. I might have found a great catch, but the day I said 'I do' was not the day I gained the entire world. I don't believe that any woman should ever look at marriage that way. Just because your husband has a master's degree does not mean that you do too. When you get married, it's true that you start sharing your life, but all the ties that bind the two of you together can be too easily broken to rely on. Say your partner has a sudden heart attack or an unexpected accident that instantly takes their life. In the blink of an eye everything you had with them is gone, now it's just what *you* have. There's no guarantee what you have left will include anything of theirs from when you were together. By then, the sting of not having an equal partnership may become a little too much to bear. My husband hates it when I say this, but one thing I know for sure is the only security a woman ever has lies in her having her own money. It's a soundness that comes for anyone with wealth. However, with women, it means so much more. With the security of her own money, a woman's life is no longer in the hands of men, but firmly planted in her own. No longer forced to live according to the whims of men who hold her life in their pockets, a woman with this kind of independence can think and do for herself in a way that is uniquely beneficial. These are impactful ideas that are distinctly female and are most often missing from much of the world of critical decision-making. They're ideas for change that tend to be more mindful of human emotions, communication, health and healthy relationships. When a woman is not given the invaluable opportunity of ownership, these ideas are all but lost forever.

Having my own money before and while I was married meant I could live without worry and love freely without the fear of what might happen to me if things unexpectedly changed. I didn't have to constantly be looking over my shoulder, waiting for the next love interest to swoop in and snatch the house I was living in from underneath me. Having my own money meant I would never be left feeling blindsided if my husband's income somehow depleted. And while we were together, as long as I was making my own money, I could make my own choices with it as well. This meant I didn't have to be restricted by how my husband thought our money should be spent. This gave me a sense of balance, power, and control. I knew that for me to be happy in my marriage, this was the kind of freedom I required.

I'd grown up in a very male-dominated culture. What I'd seen was one of the ways men around me controlled women was to keep them from having money. If the husband controlled the money, that meant he oversaw all decisions and the overall well-being of each family member. From what I'd witnessed, the woman's well-being was the last thing on his list to consider. Women who controlled their own money were not restricted. They had choice, power, and freedom in their actions and decisions. Thankfully, I believed my soon-to-be husband when he showed me that with him, these things would be guaranteed. That was all I needed to push past any reservations I might have had about shifting gears and moving in a new direction. And because of what I'd been able to do with my time before meeting my husband, I was absolutely positive I would always survive, with or without him. I had been controlling my own money, and therefore my own destiny, for years. And against the traditions of my upbringing, I saw no reason it should change just because of marriage. I would continue to maintain my independence even within my committed partnership. So I was taking a leap of faith, but it wasn't as scary as it looked from the outside. I had a sense of control over the situation that no one could ever take away from me, and that feeling was incredible.

## Navigating A New Road

You never know when you'll be faced with adversity, but when it comes, it's hard to miss. It's not something you can often ignore or run away from. Most challenges have to be faced head-on if you still want to achieve your dreams. I had no fear of moving to Cairo, Egypt. I was confident in my relationship with my fiancé and certain I was making the right choice to be with him. I had already moved twice to two different foreign countries knowing nothing of the cultures and with no one to depend on. Both times, I had risen to the occasion to fit in and made those places my home. Cairo would be the next. It would be where I found my next job, where I would be married and start my own family, and where I would start the next step of my life journey. What I found when I arrived was something I hadn't expected – the shocking, cruel reality of racism. The moment I stepped foot into the city, I felt its sting, and knew right then I'd have to find some way to work through it if I wanted to be successful.

Egypt has a very complex history of race-driven classicism that runs painfully deep. It is a country that has been multi-racial and multi-ethnic since the beginning of its existence, and a home to peoples from an abundance of cultures and various backgrounds for centuries. But presently, there's a tendency to associate Egyptian purity and beauty with the fairness of skin. And though this association isn't an uncommon phenomenon in today's society, in Egypt in particular, this has resulted in some very ugly discriminatory practices that were still alive and well when I lived there. In the capital city of Cairo, the tension stemming from these practices and the proud racist attitudes they resulted in could be cut with a knife. It was very normal for fair-skinned Egyptians to treat Black Egyptians, or anyone darker-skinned for that matter, as if they were lower in status or plain worthless. Because of this, I couldn't really get a good-paying job once I got there. Where I worked in Hurghada, it was a major tourist destination, filled with visitors creating their own kind of Egypt. There they turned Egypt into a place where people were accepting, happy, and free of judgement of any kind. Outside of those bounds of the resort, things were drastically different. From the moment I arrived in Cairo, I felt that difference. The collective thoughts, looks, and judgments of hundreds of people at a time pressing on me as I walked through the streets. Seeing their eyes narrow as I passed, or watching their mouths tighten into a thin line when I entered a store. Or voices lowering, and smiles fading as dissatisfied eyes fell upon me. For the first time in my life, because of my race, I would not be able to get a job.

Prior to my time in Cairo, I was no stranger to prejudice or discrimination. Back in Uganda, there was sexism – which I knew all too well – colorism, and even tribalism. There, someone might not give you a job because you didn't belong to the same tribe as them and not think anything of it. That's just how it was. That, I was used to. However, what I experienced in Cairo was beyond anything I'd ever witnessed. It was something completely new and far more cruelly blatant. I once saw a Black woman standing in line at the store. When it was her turn to check out, she placed her items on the counter and waited for the cashier to ring them up. The cashier, looking past her, saw a fair-skinned Egyptian standing behind her in line. The cashier told the Black woman to move her things and step aside so she could check the fair-skinned woman out first. If we went to a restaurant it wouldn't be a surprise if we had to wait longer than most to be seated and longer than normal to be served. The area where we lived had a lot of expats, so you wouldn't find as much awful behavior where we were staying, but we did have a girl who used to clean for us that would travel from out of town. One morning she arrived soaking wet and dirty, telling me that as she was walking to our home someone purposely threw a bucket of dirty water on her. Afraid that we would fire her for being late if she turned back to change her clothes, she suffered the indignity and continued on to our house. I couldn't believe someone would do something like that. Sadly with time, I grew accustomed to hearing stories like these. Being on the receiving end of dozens of painful reminders and injustices each day had conditioned me to believe that these instances were not only typical, but acceptable.

Many Africans from across the continent would go to Egypt for various reasons. To get an education, find work, enjoy the holidays, start a business, or start a whole new life. I was pursuing some of these same opportunities myself. These were all things believed to be available to citizens and foreigners alike. It's not uncommon for a young Black girl from Uganda to get a job working as a nanny, maid, or domestic person in Egypt. If she stayed home, she might be lucky to earn $50 a month for her services, but in Egypt she could make upwards of $500 a month. Some Africans were fleeing death and persecution in their own countries, seeking refuge and hoping to find a safe place to call home and begin productive lives. For them, Cairo was a haven – conveniently located and relatively easy to enter. Freedoms like these are extremely attractive and still heavily pursued on that side of the world, but the realities were harsh. Arriving in this new, promisingly just country is soured when you see families with their Black maids and nannies sitting in trunks, squeezed in the back of cars filled with bags from the day's shopping trip, and screaming kids bouncing happily in the seats ahead of them. What was most unbelievable to my husband and I wasn't that we saw this on a day to day basis, but that everyone thought it was normal.

Realizing how difficult it would be for me to find a job worth my time, my husband and I decided we would use our duration in Cairo to travel the world and have kids as we went along. At the end of his three-year contract, we'd planned to move to the US, at which point we'd have a family, and after we were finished having children, I could continue my career. I always knew I would be a mother, but I also knew how badly I desired a full-time career. And if I was going to do both, then I needed to make sure I could handle both. If we were going to live in the United States, I would have to adjust to so many new things I didn't know. Considering the fact that I would be starting and growing a business in a new country, on a different continent, with all different types of people, I knew I would have a lot to learn, juggle, and do. The added pressure of being pregnant while I did this was not something I particularly wanted, so using the rest of our time in Egypt to have all of the kids we could while I wasn't working seemed like the perfect plan.

The first thing I did when I moved in with my husband in Cairo was stay home for a little bit while I figured things out. I wanted to know what was going on in Cairo and how I could possibly capitalize on what was available. So when my husband was working and when we weren't travelling, I spent my time thinking, researching, and trying to create an opportunity for myself. It wasn't in my nature not to work, and it wasn't possible for me to relax, lead a life of leisure, and depend on my husband day in and day out. I knew there was an opportunity for me in Cairo. I just had to find it. My first idea was to buy Egyptian towels and ship them to Uganda. The towels in Cairo were extremely luxurious and I knew people would be willing to buy and pay a premium price for them. But I never really pulled the trigger on that idea. After working through the numbers, I found shipping would be ridiculous. And even if I did have potential clientele, they most likely wouldn't be willing to pay as much as I would need from them to cover those costs and for me to turn a reasonable profit. Unfortunately, it took me four or five months of research before I came to this conclusion. During that time, two exciting developments took shape. First, I became pregnant with our first son. Second, I relaunched my cake sales business. I realized there were a large number of Africans looking for cakes to be made in a traditional African style, markedly different from the standard cakes they could get in Cairo. I learned people were ordering cakes outside of Egypt for birthdays, graduations, and other celebrations. So I began making and selling African cakes just as I had when I was a child. I made a larger version of the cake to target people who were having larger gatherings and celebrations, and as suspected, my business took off. In addition to that, I began working on another opportunity. I knew the list of what people in Uganda wanted but could not get was long, so the possibilities were numerous. After considering what happened with the towel idea, I looked for something else I could export from Egypt that wouldn't require shipping. I settled on cell phones. I would buy cell phones in Egypt and sell them in Uganda. With this idea, I was able to cut out shipping by buying the phones in Egypt and carrying them on the flight with me when I flew to Uganda for my routine trips. And everything went very well. Through my cake business and cell phone sales, I once again had a healthy source of income.

It felt good not to validate the idea that because I was Black in an unwelcome place, I couldn't succeed at whatever I chose to do. It felt great to be busy, and even better to hit a new level of success as a business woman. The color of my skin could keep other people from offering me a good job, a fair wage, and an equal shot in the workforce. But it could not stop me from starting and growing my own businesses. I didn't get hung up on the thought of having to operate among some of the same people who made life so difficult for most darker-skinned people in the city. I embraced who I was and used it to my advantage. Once I realized my skin color, gender, and age could not be used to hold me back as long as I worked for myself, it gave me the sense of power and control I needed to eventually rise above the racism that plagued our years in Cairo. I cannot tell you how many times my family and I had to endure racist comments and attacks while we were living there.

One time, we went on a vacation to Thailand. It was the most perfect vacation, we really had the time of our lives. But it felt like the second we came back we were reminded of exactly what we'd left behind. While my husband waited for our luggage at the airport's baggage claim, he had struck up a friendly conversation with an Egyptian man also waiting for his luggage. My son and I weren't with him, but we were sitting nearby. I could catch parts of the conversation from where I was, and I distinctly remember hearing my husband saying something about his wife and son. I looked up to see him pointing to us as the ugliest expression I have ever seen washed over the stranger's face. "What are you doing with a Black person?!" He shouted. The man was clear and loud, and I will never forget the way his face crumpled into a scowl as his eyes fell on me. The way he said the word *black* hit my ears with a sting. He said it like he was swearing.

Another time, I was walking toward a group of Egyptian men on the street who'd been walking in the opposite direction. When our paths crossed, they started speaking Arabic. I didn't know the language, but had been picking it up bit by bit the longer I stayed in Cairo. I couldn't understand everything they were saying, but I could sense the hostility. As they got closer they spit on me, using an Arabic word I knew to be a racial slur along with a curse I also recognized. Translated loosely the word meant "corpse" and by using it these men wished me dead, casting the vision of my body lying in a grave in the cemetery. Oddly enough, my first response was not shame, fear, or anger – it was confusion. I was so surprised and still feel that way when I think about it. I couldn't even believe there were people walking around treating other people as if they were less than trash. I couldn't understand why something so clearly wrong, and obviously despicable was so acceptable. It was times like these that made me grateful for how I could look at situations that most people would get discouraged by and find the positives in them, whatever they were. There was my cake business that focused primarily on people like me in a foreign country that was doing so well. Then there was my cell phone business where I made money while I visited with family and checked on my investments. And, my ability to stay home and raise my kids - all of these things were side effects of me being in Cairo. I took the good with the bad because if I had decided that being Black was going to keep me from starting a business in Cairo, then I would have been right. Instead, I chose to use my Blackness as a way to better my situation and keep a positive perspective on my time in Egypt. I trusted I would be just as resilient as I'd always been by believing in myself and in what I could achieve. I saw the culture in Cairo for what it was and strengthened my resolve. The power and control *within* me was the only power and control *over* me. There were still moments, exchanges, and instances of abject racial cruelty that were hard to endure, but I never surrendered. These people, this place, and these circumstances would not dictate what I could do or become.

## Moving On Toward Better Things

During our years in Cairo, my husband travelled a great deal, and so did I. When he was travelling for work, I would take the four and a half hour flight to Uganda to visit and keep myself occupied. Through the years, I'd not only been sending money home to help support my family, but I'd been developing investments in property and other assets, knowing that the best use of money is to put it into something that will create more of itself. It became easy for me to do those things while he was away, so I wouldn't just be left at home waiting for him to get back. Around the time the Egyptian revolution had started to really gain momentum and spill into the streets, I was trying to get my sister to start a business back home where she'd be selling a variety of spare parts. I wanted so much for her to start creating a safety net for herself. I saw the spare parts business as a way for her to generate income and gain more power and control over her life. I desperately wanted for her what I'd created for myself, so I was making trips to Uganda fairly frequently.

When I started living with my husband, I'd always make sure I kept the house stocked with food, almost overbuying – a possible side effect of my childhood. I guess I never really felt secure with food even though my husband had a good job and I was earning a decent living on my own. We were nowhere close to starving. I just kept feeling like we would run out of food if I didn't make the effort to buy enough. So, I would buy a lot more than we needed, which meant my husband rarely had to do the grocery shopping. It took many years for my food insecurity to recede. Most days, I'd cook and pack the meals in the fridge or freezer so he'd always have something to heat up and eat, even if I wasn't around. This one particular trip, I was going to Uganda but my husband was staying at home. Looking for something to keep himself busy while I was gone, he asked me not to buy any food for the house before I left so he could do the shopping himself if he needed anything (which he would not). I agreed and left for my trip that same day. That night after I'd settled in, I texted to check up on him. I wanted to let him know I was okay and that my flight was fine, but more importantly, I wanted to make sure he was serious about feeding himself. But he never replied. I thought it was a bit strange, but at that moment, I didn't feel like it was a big deal. I wasn't worried. I just thought maybe he was busy, caught up in work or something else. *Maybe he did end up going grocery shopping.* He would get back to me when he was free. The next day when I woke up and still hadn't heard anything from him, I started to worry. I'd spent the entire day prior out having fun and catching up with friends, so I didn't have any idea of what was going on in Egypt. I hadn't had the time to sit down and read the news or catch any reports on TV, but I'd felt something was not right. I called my husband's office that night, hoping to catch him there, but still no answer. That's when I learned the uprising was fully underway across the country. All phone service, internet connection, and everything needed for communications between the citizens staying in Cairo and the rest of the world was severed.

I wasn't living in Egypt when the revolution initially started, but the way everything turned out, it was almost like I had landed one day and the rebellion started the next. By the beginning of 2011, two years after I'd relocated to Egypt, demonstrations had broken out in the city of Cairo as well as several different cities across the country. Thousands of protesters were flooding the streets, and hundreds of people were being beaten, arrested, injured, and killed, all while they spoke up against police brutality and a host of other issues imposed by the Egyptian government. Now, the country was in full revolt. My son and I were stuck in Uganda and I had no idea where his father was. My heart, stomach, and head pounded with panic. I felt hysterical inside. But I could not give in to it. This was a problem I needed to work through and solve methodically and thoughtfully. After a few calls, I learned that my husband's company had started evacuating their employees to France, so by then I was just hoping to hear from him and find out if he was safely out of the country and okay. But there was no way of knowing for sure whether or not he'd been evacuated until we could get in contact with one another. There was a strong possibility he was still in Cairo, thinking that I was only supposed to be in Uganda for a few days. I had a thought he might be worried that my trip was so short I would return to Cairo, find he wasn't there, then be stuck with a revolution raging around me, which wasn't something he'd want me to face alone. I remember nothing from this time other than the silence of my phone and my desperate desire for it to ring. About a week later when we finally spoke for the first time since I'd left, I learned he really did end up staying in Egypt waiting for me. The company had brought a plane to take all of their employees out, but he didn't go. I was thinking it was crazy that he'd do that, but I was relieved he was safe. The stockpiles of food I left for him had kept him comfortable the entire time. At that point, my husband contacted the US Embassy. Being an American citizen, we figured we could rely on their assistance to get him out of the country. Fortunately, I had my US visa, so from there we came up with a plan and moved as quickly as we could. As soon as my husband left Egypt, my son and I left Uganda, and we all met in Amsterdam. From there, we went straight to the US where we stayed for 30 days, until things calmed down. Once Mubarak stepped down and things kind of settled, we decided it was safe to move back. But by then, it was like everything had been turned upside down.

Prior to the uprising, the streets of Cairo were typically filled with police. You couldn't walk for more than two straight blocks without seeing them patrolling. Once we returned, we saw that there were virtually no police anywhere. It was an eerie reminder of why the demonstrations had broken out in the first place, and it left us wondering if things would ever be the same. We were also hearing horror stories of awful crimes being committed. Terrible crimes against Blacks. Stories of countless bodies, especially those of Black Africans, being found in the desert missing their kidneys, hearts, and some other major organs. Big piles of Black bodies spilling out of holes feverishly dug in the sands. Black people, found in their cars completely slaughtered by machete on the sides of roads – roads that were a mere mile away from where we lived at the time. It was all so unsettling. My husband was openly worried about my safety, and for the first time in my life, I began to fear too. Me, the same person who walked the streets at the age of 10 shrugging off witch doctors as children my age were being snatched up and butchered. Also the same me who relocated executed bodies from the dungeon cells of the palace to make a safe place to roast and eat stolen food. Suddenly the possibility of harm or death felt very real. Knowledge of these things was precisely what made us even more anxious to relocate as soon as possible. With that on my mind, I remained fixated on what life would be like once we did.

## If The Dress Fits...

A little before this when my oldest was just six months old, my husband and I agreed to have his baptism party in Kampala so he could meet my side of the family and get better acquainted. As we were visiting, I decided I would buy my dress for the party there instead of in Cairo. It wasn't that I couldn't buy a dress in Cairo because I most definitely could have. There were a number of malls there and I knew exactly where to look, but for whatever my reasoning, I decided on shopping in Kampala. Unfortunately, when I started shopping for a dress in the city, I had an extremely difficult time finding exactly what I was looking for. Any woman who's ever had a baby can understand just how I was feeling. I was so insecure about my body, and it took me the whole day to find a dress. I went downtown looking in so many shops trying to find the perfect dress. By the end of the day, I was so exhausted, I just settled on something I didn't really like all that much. All of the dresses I looked at were either too expensive for the occasion or they didn't make me feel comfortable. None fit the way that I hoped. Looking at the dress I chose and thinking about how hard it was to find something I barely liked for a reasonable price, I got the idea for the business I would eventually start when we moved to the United States. In cities like Cairo, London, and all over the US, there were malls full of shops and department stores with dresses in every size, fit, and color. The options were endless in those places. *Imagine if I could bring those options here.*

I wanted to open a store that only sold dresses. From work, cocktail, party, red carpet, every type of dress there was, we would sell it. But that was only the beginning of my vision. I wanted for people to think of my store anytime they ever thought of buying a dress in Kampala. It would have the best selection, best quality, and options you couldn't find anywhere else. From my research on importing towels from Cairo, I knew that starting this dress company would not be possible when I'd had the idea. I would need to be in a place where the inventory was expansive, and the shipping costs were minimal. It was a great idea, but the timing was not right, so I continued to pour my focus into my cake and cell phone businesses.

During the last year we lived in Egypt, months before we even moved to the US, I began preparing myself to adapt to another new country. Following the birth of my daughter, I would be starting over again with two children under the age of two. My goals were still the same, and I anticipated I would encounter the same barriers I had faced in the past. My husband still had his job, which he would continue doing after our relocation to the US, but I would not be able to find a job or work for someone else. Not with two small children, likely a third, and fourth to follow, and the complicated system of work permits I'd have to navigate in order to find legal, good-paying employment. We were moving there earlier than we initially thought we would when we were first married, so I began brainstorming ideas for businesses I could easily start and grow while raising my two children. It would need to be something that wasn't too time consuming, that didn't create stress or exert me physically, and could be done with two toddlers tagging along everywhere I went. My mind drifted back to the dress shop, and the idea quickly began taking a more defined shape. I knew clothing in the US was abundant and competitively priced. I also knew that shipping from the US to Uganda was reasonable. My understanding and command of social media would make it possible for me to market, build a customer base, and even arrange sales without physically being there. I believed that with the business model I had in mind, I could net $5k a month after all expenses were paid, allowing me to bring in $60k a year. At the time, I felt that was a good number for me to be making in addition to my husband's income. I look back now at what I'd hoped to accomplish and can't believe how much I undershot my potential!

The funny thing about that idea is that I don't even wear dresses all that much. I'm more of a t-shirt and jeans kind of girl. I never spent time fantasizing about fashion other than wanting more shoes than I could wear as a barefoot child walking through the streets of my Ugandan neighborhood. Retail was not a passion of mine, but this idea made sense for my life and the lives of most women I knew. I was positive it would work. Even funnier was that I had spent my whole life in Uganda before and had never thought of something like it until that day. There were no shops in Kampala that sold American-style plus-size dresses, yet there were many people who wanted them and would overpay to get them. I'd found the gap in the market, and now there was nothing more to do than take the necessary steps to fill it. I was simply following the money, and I trusted my instincts and expertise as an entrepreneur to see it through. These same instincts led me to start feeding my family when I was 10 years old. They had also led me to London where I'd created many opportunities for myself after moving straight from my hometown without knowing anything about the city. And lastly, my instincts had led me to Egypt where I not only found the love of my life, but had also used what little I had to make a killing with my new enterprises. I was barely over the age of 21, yet I had so many successful business ventures under my belt, and I was continuing to come up with new and lucrative ideas that anyone could carry out for themselves. Ideas I knew were valuable and valid because I had spent over half my life researching their markets and watching them work. It was just the way I looked at the world. I was always searching for innovative ways to improve my surroundings with the way my mind processed what was around me. And not just for myself, but for everyone in them. Business ideas came to me all the time, but there was something special about the dress shop. I didn't want it to just stay in my head. There would be no store in Kampala like the one I planned on opening because there weren't any in existence when I thought of the concept. If there were any then, I knew that they wouldn't have the same type of dresses I would have to offer, the variety I planned to have on hand or the same kind of branding I would market. From all the years I'd spent filling the needs of the people in that city, I was confident I had the perfect idea. I knew it would be something altogether different. Something big. When it was finally time to leave Egypt and relocate to the US, the path was there and the steps were clear. All that was left for me to do, besides get settled into my new country, was follow them.

# PART III:
# The American Dream

CHAPTER 6

# How To Build An Empire

### A lesson on starting a business

On June 1, 2012, I landed at JFK airport in New York City from Cairo, Egypt. During the three and a half years I'd lived in Cairo, it seemed like my life had changed even faster than when I lost my father. Stepping off the plane, I was now 22 years old and a wife, mother, sponsor, and successful entrepreneur. I'd become so much more than the girl I left behind in Africa roughly five years prior. I'd married a man I loved and felt supported by, and our son and daughter were happy and healthy toddlers. With the money I was making from my investments and enterprises, I regularly sent funds to my family and set up ways for them to increase their incomes. This provided them with a kind of stability and security they could never find in Uganda on their own. And as I gained more experience over time, I'd developed a proven strategy for creating, maintaining, and growing small side hustles into lucrative income streams, giving me consistent profits regardless of what kind of environment I found myself in. I'd achieved so much by the time I reached the US, it felt like I was living in my dreams. The moment my feet hit the soil, I felt instantly unburdened. Untethered. I was physically feeling the rush of success as if I were already a millionaire with multiple international enterprises. It was exciting and fulfilling. I felt accomplished, but I had no doubt there was still so much more to do and see. There were no limits to what I could accomplish in this place.

## Grasping The Vision

Since I've begun coaching women in entrepreneurship, I recognize that one of the concepts most find difficult to grasp is the importance of visualization. It is nearly impossible to become a successful person if you're unable to picture yourself as one. It isn't enough to just think it, you must visualize it with such detail it becomes real to you. What you will be wearing, what you will be driving, where you will live, how you will speak and interact, how you will present yourself to others, how they will respond to you, what you will do in your free time – the picture of your future, successful self needs to be very clear. You should be able to see yourself in your mind as if you are watching a movie of a person you would love to be. *What has this person accomplished? What have they achieved?* More than seeing them you must feel what it's like to be them. Then, with the vision of this person in your mind, start to obsess over that vision. Spend time looking at them in your mind, noticing every facet of their existence. Live as though the picture is a certainty – a conclusion rather than a possibility. A transformation that *will* happen, not *might* happen. Then all that remains is for you to keep moving forward until these images become real. I'd been envisioning my future self in many ways for as long as I could remember. I'd dedicated myself to living as if the vision in my mind was certain. This is what made the experience of succeeding in what I'd pictured so surreal. Arriving in the United States was more than a wish I hoped would one day happen. It was something I had envisioned for years, feeling the reality of each moment as I opened my mind to what could be. My relocation to the US was something I first created in my imagination, then manifested with my own action and direction. I was excited when I arrived, of course, but not surprised. I'd made it happen.

With anything you would like to accomplish, as long as you have a clear goal in mind, you have everything it takes to achieve it. If you remain focused and dedicated to your vision, all the pieces will eventually come together. The only thing that separates you from what you want is the steps you have to take to reach it. You may not know what steps to take right away, in fact, you might not figure out which actions were the right ones until after they've been made, but that should never keep you from moving forward. When you have a clear goal in mind, the plan for achieving that goal always reveals itself. Some parts of the destination you must create on your own, and some depend on finding and taking opportunities that arise along the way. But the key to staying on course and achieving the outcomes you envision is to focus to the point of obsession. This will allow you to avoid, or eliminate altogether, the things which could potentially take you off track. This is the approach I use as a primary component in my business development and for reaching life goals. For instance, as a child, I didn't spend my time playing or sleeping in on weekends. I knew these things would take me off course to earning money, which I needed to survive and earn more to eventually leave Uganda and become wealthy and successful. When you have a clear vision of what you want in the future, one that you can feel as if it's real, it's easier to avoid temptations and stay the course to fulfill it.

All the days and nights I spent imagining those elaborate scenes in my mind where I was a young millionaire – scenes where I was free to make my own decisions and control my destiny – it felt like those thoughts were my reality. And that's what felt so surreal as I stepped down from the plane. When I dreamt about what I wanted, I would always feel like I already had it. But reality said that only time could tell. While I worked hard and waited for my efforts to accumulate, I grasped whatever satisfaction I could from my daydreams. Whatever I hoped for was already mine. Believing in that felt good while I navigated my present circumstances. Even if, on the surface, it seemed like I was pretending and telling stories, I was actually making sense of what I saw, which made what I imagined more than just a daydream. I saw myself as a wife, mother, sister, friend, and wealthy businesswoman who'd made $1 million by their 25th birthday and was highly committed to sharing her wealth. This someone would have multiple successful businesses in a free country full of life-changing opportunities. This future person would be well respected by everyone they knew and praised for their ambitions and accomplishments. The person in my mind who I wanted to become had built an empire, so my present person was watching closely. And now, here I was in America. I'd never dreamt of things falling into place exactly as they had, but that wasn't my concern. The day I stepped off that plane in New York City, I'd checked another box on the list of things that would turn the movie in my mind into a scene in real life. I could not have specifically predicted the path, but I did know where it would lead. Because throughout my life, I'd been working my way backward, planning based on my end goals, and figuring out the full blueprint as I went along.

Our goals should have several components to visualize and measure so we know for sure when we've met them. As we work our way backward from the plans in our minds, the gaps of our stories become filled in. We continue to make sense of what we see as we check off the boxes to our goals while time plays out for us in our everyday lives. In my dream life, I had to be a married matriarch with close family ties. *Check.* I needed to be a businesswoman. *Check.* I needed to live in a country like the US because that's where my businesses were in my dreams. *Check.* Next on the list was creating those businesses, and growing them to bring my family and me great wealth and a lasting legacy. This was something that still had to be done. So, instead of falling under the spell of checking off boxes, I got started on the next. Just like I'd done before in London and Egypt, not even a week after I landed in America, I was already getting well acquainted with the ways of building a successful enterprise. And exactly 30 days to the day after I'd landed, I'd officially launched Ansell Dresses – the cornerstone of my empire.

## All Big Ideas Require Even Bigger Dreams

Some of the world's biggest businesses started with the simplest of ideas. Most of the time, the concepts that shape these businesses aren't called "big" ideas until they become a "big" business. It's not the magnitude of the idea itself, but how far you plan to take it.

When I moved to the US, I didn't want to have several small ventures and side hustles running at once. Eventually, I hoped to work my way up and create an empire that could sustain my family for generations and turn me into the millionaire I'd always dreamt of becoming. I needed to settle on one idea I could grow into one large business. Every business, no matter how big or small, starts with one single idea. That's all it takes. Just one thought. One hope for change, one deep-seated emotion that motivates you into action – that's all that stands between you and a different life and world. But you have to find that idea first. I had the idea for starting my dress business about a year before we moved out of Cairo, but as I took in the sights of my new home, the same idea burned brightly in my mind as if it was still brand new. I could imagine my long day shopping in Kampala, looking for the party dress I would eventually settle on, more out of exhaustion instead of excitement. I could still see, as clear as day, the handful of dresses on the racks with a meager size and style range. I went in and out of store after store, never finding the kind of dress I would easily be able to find in one of the malls in Cairo and probably for an even better price than I'd paid. I was sure that I wasn't the only woman who'd been through that sort of ordeal before, so I knew there were many others already looking for what I was thinking about bringing to life.

Finding business ideas has never really been something I struggled with, so the idea for Ansell Dresses came fairly quickly. Whether it was a need I could fill or a problem I could solve, I've always understood that there are endless ideas. My mind works like an entrepreneur. What separates an entrepreneur from others is that they not only see problems, but see themselves as the solution. Others see the issue and think, "I wish there was someone or something to fix that." I was constantly thinking of new ways of making money to the point where there were things I knew would work, but I just never attempted the startups because I didn't have the time or circumstances to see them through. For me, business ideas are easy to come by. However, there are plenty of people out there that say to themselves they would like to start a business, but then stop right there because they can't zero in on what that business should be. Sometimes ideas will pop into your head, and they automatically make sense, which is fantastic. But if that rarely happens for you, start small. Take out a sheet of paper and brainstorm.

Instead of reinventing the wheel or coming up with something the world has never seen before, simply think about what *you* can offer. With my business ideas, I usually start with what I know, taking into account my lists of interests, hobbies, and skills, then finding a way to use those characteristics to fill a hole I've seen in the market. Often, you can think of day-to-day frustrations and how you might be able to alleviate them. As a child, school transportation was unreliable and expensive because it relied on independent public drivers who didn't operate according to routes or a schedule. So, I coordinated a group of students, collected their fare, booked the vehicle, negotiated a rate for less than the total amount of each rider, and got a free ride for myself. Other ideas came from the people around me, simply telling me what they wanted and needed. This is what happened when I first started making candles. In this situation, the idea wasn't necessarily my own, but I trusted it because it came from the very people who could be my first customers.

A lot of times, you can look around at your environment and think about what can be improved upon and how you can do that with a business of your own. Are there any products or services missing from the market you're immersed in that you can provide? Think of any day-to-day frustrations you or other people you know might have and how to alleviate or eliminate them. Most times, you can do what other people are already doing. Whatever is working for their business, use it to work for your own, making sure you customize the concept for the community you hope to serve. Think of companies like Amazon and Walmart. All they've done is buy a bunch of things and sell them in one place. How many times has that been done throughout history? Countless. It's where they went from there that's impressive. Think of Uber – people with cars sharing rides with people without cars. This was not a new idea. We already have taxis. But look at what they created by introducing that idea in an entirely new way. This was the basis of my idea for Ansell Dresses. Figuring out what you want to do is just the first step in starting a business, so you can't let it trip you up or stop you completely in your tracks because there's still so much more work to be done after.

When I had my idea for Ansell Dresses, it was simple enough, but my vision of the future and what I wanted to do with it was much bigger than just selling dresses. This was because I had my dreams to take into consideration. My life goals were huge, so by default, any ideas I had would have to fit this particular outlook I'd held for the way things would eventually turn out for me. If you do not dream big, you will not win big – simple as that. An idea for a multi-million dollar company will have a hard time being formed in a mind that doesn't believe making millions of dollars is possible. You must condition yourself to think bigger, as big as you can. Think of the things that scare you, the things that might seem impossible for anyone to accomplish, and visualize yourself doing them. Imagine a world where you are invincible, where you can have, do, and be anything you want. In doing this, your reality will start to follow suit, giving you those simple ideas that lead you to your greatest dreams. It takes practice to think like an entrepreneur. But as I've said before, the idea phase of starting a business is only the beginning. Once I had my idea, I needed to figure out how I'd get it up and running.

## If You Don't Know What To Do, Find Someone Who Does

When you're first starting to do anything you've never done before, finding someone else who's done it already is your best bet. Taking the time to learn from a mentor or a previously executed business model similar to yours is a foolproof way to make all the right decisions and avoid all the wrong things that can bring difficulties. Someone's already made all the mistakes for you. Let them lead by example and mimic what they've done as carefully as possible. Using their experiences, you can begin to build on your imagination, and then their journey of clawing their way to the top can become your springboard. Instead of starting from scratch, you'll have some of the answers you might've been searching for, some of the questions you might've never thought to ask, and a clear example to follow and modify as needed. And no matter how uncommon your idea may be, there's always someone out there or some event in the past you can relate to and learn from. You've just got to seek them out. At first, it may feel intimidating or like it's too much work, but sometimes finding them is even easier than we think.

From the day we settled in our new home in Pittsburgh, Pennsylvania, I felt the energy of possibilities. Of course, I was excited to learn about the culture and the people, but more than anything, I was interested in learning as much as I could about business. Mostly how the people in my newly adopted country ran their companies. In Kampala, things were completely different, and they were just as different in London, Hurghada, and Cairo. I wanted to know exactly how people studied business concepts and ran their enterprises in the United States. The quicker I started a business in the States, the faster my dollars would add up to enough Ugandan shillings to keep my family taken care of for generations. But I didn't know much about the country, at least not anything that could help me start a successful business, so it was imperative that I found a way to get the answers I needed. The fact I knew nothing didn't discourage me or deter me at all. Having no idea how I would accomplish what I hoped wasn't a stopping point, it was a starting point. The first place I started was Google. I began looking for and finding others who had done perfectly well what I was hoping to do. In the absence of someone I could speak with over the phone or meet physically, I had social media postings, online articles, and books filled with stories of triumph and failure. When I searched the phrase 'business TV shows and movies,' one of the first results was *Shark Tank*. I started watching almost immediately, and before I even finished my first episode, I was hooked.

On *Shark Tank*, expert entrepreneurs shared their knowledge of American businesses and how they were traditionally run. This happened once a week on national television for the price of a monthly basic cable subscription. You could even watch clips of the episodes for free on YouTube! I could hardly believe it. I got to hear the types of questions people were asking, what the sharks were thinking, and all the startup stories I could ever imagine. Watching *Shark Tank* helped me to understand how businesses worked in the US and how to sell them to the market. More importantly, it pointed to the concepts I still needed to research and understand. All the information was helpful, entertaining, and most importantly, affordable. From there, I went to social media, and I followed all the sharks from the show. I consumed every scrap of information I could about them. Then I added all the biggest business media outlets like Entrepreneur Magazine, Business Insider, and Forbes. Basically, anything having to do with business, I was seeking out and paying close attention. That's when I realized I wasn't alone. I wasn't the only person that thought the way I did. There were a lot of other people that looked at the world the same way as me. We were all continually finding ideas to improve our lives and the lives of others; always searching for ways to make money so we could use it to make more. I felt seen.

Discovering *Shark Tank* was like finding my place in a world I didn't realize existed. Here were these billionaire expert entrepreneurs openly sharing their knowledge about business ventures and start-ups, and there I was thinking, "Well yes, of course," and "He's right, that'll never work." I was amazed at how on point my instincts were and how aligned my mind was to theirs. While I was growing up, I didn't even know why I had most of the thoughts I had. But hearing people like Mark Cuban say some of the same things I would say to myself, validated how my mind worked and who I was as a person. Here I was, this kid that hadn't gone to college, coming from Africa with all these little side hustles, thinking almost exactly the same as Mark Cuban himself. When I heard him say, "passion is bullshit," I lost it. I went crazy. I'd never understood why passion was necessary, not even as I watched this Ivy League business graduate cry about hers on that episode. For me, it had always been about the money. And here was Shark Tank delving into the concept. I was overjoyed. After all those years of chasing the money and being successful at it, none of that meant so much until I heard Mark Cuban say those three words. The majority of enterprises I created up to that point didn't have much to do with my interests outside of making money, and I wasn't ashamed or burned out because of it. I'd enjoyed eating popcorn, but it wasn't my life's work. I wasn't particularly passionate about finding scrap metal. I didn't love making candles, and I didn't have an emotional desire to bake cakes. Until, of course, I got paid for these things, then I was happy. I learned very early on I didn't need passion to be successful or to enjoy my rewards. I just needed a goal to meet and the drive to get there. Everything I believed about making money, building businesses, investing – all of that was instantly validated when I discovered *Shark Tank*. I wasn't out of my mind. I was just an entrepreneur. Hearing all the things I'd held in my heart for so long echoed right back to me, I knew for sure, I was moving in the right direction.

I was amazed that all these people I'd never seen before and didn't even know were putting words to these feelings I'd followed all my life but could never articulate. In fact, I'd never tried. It had never occurred to me that people needed to like what they were doing. It just made more sense to focus on how much money I could make instead of how much I liked to do any of the things that brought it to me. Because everybody wants money, they just don't admit it freely. Everyone uses the word "success" instead. Success brings freedom, then when you're free, you have the power. But success can only be measured by so many things. The thing that contributes to your business success is the money it makes. Money is your measurement. On *Shark Tank*, money is the most crucial part of the conversation. When you're presenting your business to the sharks, it doesn't matter how great your idea is or how long your company has been around. What matters is how much money you've made and spent, how much the business will make, and how much the sharks have to pay to get in. Because it's not what you have, but what can be done with it.

Think about it. Wouldn't you give $500 to someone who promises to triple your investment instead of giving $1500 to someone who promises to keep it safe for you? Someone who can triple $500 can do the same with any amount. But people who don't know how to do that just count the days until they run out of funds. Money is the easiest thing you can place goals on because it's already numbered. You just have to count it and watch where it goes. It may have to come into your hands, but once you get it, you can put your money to work for you and instantly start making more. Hold on to money, and it dwindles away. Let it move thoughtfully, and it multiplies. Fortunately, I'd spent many years developing a money mindset that made making and multiplying my cash easy. As long as I had a plan to follow and a number in mind, it was just a matter of steps before I got the amount I was looking for.

## Never Go Into Anything Completely Blind

Think of a blind man standing at the edge of a dense forest, a dying city to his back. The man is stubborn, lives alone, and trusts no one. But he's heard whispers of a beautiful paradise in the middle of the very forest that stands before him. He knows for sure that paradise is close enough to get to on foot, only three short miles away, and the resources there are almost endless. He's overheard people saying that life in paradise is perfect and to go there is entirely free. The man is hungry, tired, bitter, and broke, but still hoping for better, so he's jumped to action and now faces quite possibly the greatest challenge of his life. With no prior knowledge of his surroundings other than understanding that he must go through the forest in front of him if he wants to reach the safe haven inside, he sets off alone. Believing it best not to reveal his motives to anyone who may want to sabotage his journey, the man trusts himself to walk in a straight line led only by his other working senses and what little he knows of landscapes like these. As he begins traveling through the forest, feeling his way through the foreign environment, the man's smooth, confident walk bred from his life in the city now turns into a clumsy stumble. Without the slightest clue of what's in front of him until the moment he's faced with it, the man can barely take two steps without stopping and strategizing his path. After three grueling days of having to create winding detours each time his planned straight line led to walls of rock or massive holes in the ground, the man finally makes it to paradise. His body aching and scarred from a demanding trip, he hobbles to the entrance and takes in the feeling of finally being out of the woods. Moved to tears, he begins to cry. Almost immediately, a gatekeeper for the place sees the man, grabs him gently by the arm, and says, "Sorry sir, we've just closed for the weekend, but you can buy your ticket for next week's activities on our website. Now please, wait here while I call our complimentary cab service to take you back to the city."

Research is fundamental, but most people tend to neglect it. They get an idea and have this feeling it's going to work, so they jump in headfirst. And that's not always a bad thing. You never want to waste any time getting started, and you don't want to second-guess yourself. But when you go into anything blind without a well-thought-out plan, it makes the journey that much more difficult. Technically, you'll always be going in blind with anything new you wish to accomplish and experience. The fact that it's so new means you have no idea what to expect from the pursuit or achievement of what you're hoping to see. But when you make an effort to get to know more about what you're getting yourself into, you gain valuable foresight. Figuring out how to avoid anything that will keep you from reaching your goals as quickly as possible is a crucial part of the preparation and execution of your plans. When it comes to starting a business, your research makes that path clear. With a clear path, your idea will become more easily developed and carried out. In the case of the blind man, had he spoken to just one person in the city he was trying so desperately to escape, or asked one question of the place of paradise, his journey may have only taken the few minutes it was meant to instead of the three days it did. He would've found out that only getting there was free, but purchasing a ticket had a price tag all its own. And he probably would've also learned how it was better not to go so close to the weekend. Simply put, research is a form of help that most of us can't afford to ignore. By allowing what you've investigated and learned to help you create the plan you have for your business, there is less room for surprises and more opportunities for success.

When it came to my research for Ansell Dresses, I knew that Ugandans loved products from the US because of the quality. It was true that most things were made in China. But the Chinese garments shipping to America compared to those that shipped straight to Uganda were, for lack of a better phrase, cut from a different cloth. The difference is so vast that people in Uganda will gladly pay top dollar for used clothing coming from America rather than new clothing shipped directly to Uganda. This meant I would have no problem selling. I'd have the advantage over every other potential retailer because I would supply garments sourced only from the US. According to what I'd seen on my shopping trip nearly a year before, I also knew there was a significant gap in the Ugandan market for the specific kinds of dresses I now had access to. Finally, I knew there was a limited customer base, because there are a limited number of people with disposable income in Kampala. But those who had money *had money*, and they would gladly pay for quality. I knew if I attracted these customers and provided quality and selection, I could capture the market. All these observations came from my own experiences, but there was so much more I didn't have the slightest clue about. For starters, I didn't know exactly where I was going to buy the dresses. Then there was the question of how much I could charge when I sold them. Then, I thought about how much money I'd have to spend on shipping. I also wondered how I'd deliver the orders to my customers without any issues or delays.

Google is an unsung hero. It gives a clear answer for anything you ask it. Even if it can't give you a complete answer, it at least points you in the direction of finding what you're looking for. That's truly an amazing thing. With the invention of the internet and high-powered search engines like Google, the same information that's turned so many people into millionaires and billionaires in the past has today become fast and free in most places around the globe. However, when faced with a challenging question or situation, most people just say 'I don't know' and forget about research altogether. They give up because they're intimidated by the thought of finding a solution instead of just taking the time to search for it. Getting comfortable with research, asking questions, and solving problems are all valuable characteristics of an entrepreneur. In the mind of an entrepreneur, 'I don't know' quickly transforms into 'how do I figure this out?' A large part of being an entrepreneur and starting your own business is understanding that you won't know everything right away. You don't need to. Eventually, you will find out precisely what you'll need to know and do to accomplish your goals. But only if you start by searching for the answers will they be revealed.

## Make A Plan That Makes Cents

There's a great quote in the book *Rich Dad, Poor Dad* that illustrates the mindset most people have about building wealth. The author Robert Kiyosaki writes, "If you are going to build the Empire State Building, the first thing you need to do is dig a deep hole and pour a strong foundation. If you are going to build a home in the suburbs, all you need to do is pour a six-inch slab of concrete. In their drive to get rich, most people are trying to build an Empire State Building on a six-inch slab." That quote says it all. Prepare properly and you will position your business for considerable growth. Cut corners, rush or fail to fully understand your product, market, customers, and potential, and you will not build much. More likely, you won't sustain at all. There's this idea amongst most people that they can see the big dreams they have without first building the correct foundation for them to exist and last outside their minds. You can hope and dream and pray all you want, but if you do not correctly prepare what's needed to allow that dream to endure outside of yourself, then what you've built was doomed from the beginning. It's not at all sustainable to create something you are not yet ready to maintain.

In many ways, the time between your research and launch is the foundation that Robert mentioned in his book. It's a time when you put everything into place to carry out the actions needed to build the great wealth you hope to see. For example, if you learned it would be more cost-effective to: buy a bicycle for delivering your handmade flower arrangements, then next you would purchase the bike, map out your potential routes, buy the supplies, schedule arrangements and deliveries, etc. The setup also includes budgeting and scheduling, which gives you an idea of what kind of cash and time you will need to start and keep things running smoothly. Not every business plan is going to be the same. Some projects can be straightforward, while others might need to be highly complex. A plan to start a lemonade stand would be simple compared to a plan to start a restaurant, but there are a few core things that every founder should give attention to when they're making plans to launch.

## Branding

I knew that just selling clothing in Kampala was not, on its own, a winning strategy. Having a product or service for sale does not guarantee you'll make money unless people buy it. Choosing to build a business in an already oversaturated market makes selling even more challenging. When you have to compete with other companies that offer nearly identical solutions to yours, differentiating what you have to offer as unique to your business becomes the only way to turn a reasonable profit in a market full of customers with options. There were plenty of dress stores in Kampala that sold beautiful dresses in all styles. I needed to create a brand if I wanted to stand out. Branding may not be essential to start up, but it is crucial to longevity. Having consumers know and remember you is most crucial if you want them to buy multiple times. With a distinct brand, your target market can be influenced to seek out your business for whatever it is you offer, even if others can equally meet their needs. Having a strong brand drives customers to begin thinking of your business as the only one that can provide them with what they want, and how they want it. It's the same reason people go to McDonald's for a cheeseburger on their lunch break. Customers don't go because they think they're going to eat the best burger ever. They go because they are sure it will be inexpensive. They also know the menu is simple enough for them to memorize and decide on before they get to the counter or drive-thru window. Their service is consistent and predictable. When most people dine at McDonald's, the most common understanding is that their trip will be quick, taking less than 15 minutes to order and eat, leaving them worry-free about losing time and money. When they have more time and money, maybe these people will eat someplace else. But for situations like this, hungry people with little time and less cash can look for the golden arches and red roof because they already know what to expect when they get there. And that's exactly what branding does. It builds trust between the business and its consumers so that in time, those who choose to buy will always buy because of what they believe they'll be getting from the seller in addition to the products or services they offer.

    A strong brand should begin with a purpose or story that draws in the buyer and makes them want to spend their money with you only. A good rule of thumb is to communicate the why behind the business. What are the major reasons why you started the venture in the first place? Who are you looking to serve? What problems are you looking to solve? Once you know for sure what makes your business different from every other business like yours, embrace it fully and figure out how to communicate this identity with your potential and existing customers. Figure out a way to ensure that people are made aware of your business, they already know what it stands for and what it can deliver. Most businesses begin branding with strategically designed names and logos, characterized by colors and shapes that are scientifically proven to catch the eyes and stay on consumers' brains in their target markets. This is something that works. Some of the most recognizable and successful brands today have made millions off the strength of their logos alone. Consider big names like Target department stores and the designer brand Chanel. When people see the red bullseye belonging to the general retailer, they automatically think of everything on their shopping lists they still have left to buy and are reminded that Target is the place to get it all. When people see the double C's representing Chanel's fashions, they recall the founder, her minimalist designs, and their luxurious and timeless style.

Other businesses develop their brand strategies through thoughtful business models, instantly positioning themselves as establishments that fill holes in the market to which they hope to belong. In doing this, the need for bright signs and catchy slogans goes away because the end-user the business wishes to serve is already waiting for that business to exist. When a business is branded this way, its customers become customers out of sheer necessity. Knowing they have no one else to turn to, your business will inevitably gain the loyalty of those particular people. This brings guaranteed buyers and lasting profits as long as no other business comes around offering what you've been offering. It's the reason why brands like Coca-Cola have stood the test of time and continue to grow. Because of their proprietary recipe that made up the brand's first product, there's no other soda on the market that tastes like theirs. That means there's no other place for Coca-Cola's customers to go for the taste they've grown to love other than their brand. When I was building my dress business, these were the types of strategies I studied. I wanted to build a level of recognition that spoke to my store's identity, what it offered, and what it would deliver.

I knew from the beginning I wanted people to think of my store whenever they thought about buying a dress in Uganda. To make sure this happened, I needed to have strong brand recognition. When people bought from me, they'd know exactly what to expect. They would feel compelled to share and could clearly communicate to their friends and families what they'd be able to find in my store. This would bring me more customers through word of mouth. I wanted my store to be *the* place to buy dresses. Something that felt exclusive. When women asked each other where they bought their dresses, I wanted them to name my store with pride. My target market was young working women who were socialite types, women who wore nice dresses for nights out, birthday parties, office work, and everything in between. Kampala is pretty small compared to most major cities, so if these women were buying from me, I wanted to make sure that even if they attended the same events, they'd never be caught wearing the same dress as someone else in their social scenes. To ensure this was possible, I decided I would only sell one of each dress. This would become the foundation of my brand. To this day, it's something I have never done differently.

Having a good name was important too, but I'm not that great with coming up with names for my businesses, to tell the truth. What generally happens is I don't settle on something until right before I launch and am forced to write something on the website or the legal entity documents. This is essentially what ended up happening with my dress shop, so I kept it simple – Ansell Dresses. From the name alone, people got the idea of what we sold and who we were. It wasn't too complicated to remember and was unique enough not to forget. The logo was equally unforgettable. Clean, clear and simple. An interconnected A and D, sharp and fitted but at the same time flowing and beautiful. The shop's name spelled out underscored the two. I felt it visually captured our identity and purpose perfectly. We would focus on plus-size dresses, which tended to be scarce in stores despite the many women around who fit those sizes. We would be their solution. With Ansell Dresses, these women could be assured they'd find beautiful, stylish, one-of-a-kind garments that were imported but not outside of their budgets or reach. There wasn't any other dress business in Kampala making those kinds of promises with that kind of inventory. It would be an inclusive yet distinctive experience to shop with us. It was apparent that Ansell Dresses would stand out, but only after everyone knew it was there. For this, I moved on to my marketing strategy.

## Marketing

Marketing is the simple promotion of your business' products or services to its target market. There's no point in starting a business if you're not going to tell anybody about it, so marketing is a big part of your setup. Being remembered through branding is necessary, but you have to be seen before you can be remembered. Letting people know your business exists is crucial to your initial success. It seems simple enough until we consider the number of owners who've opened their operations with ringing bells and blowing whistles only to hear crickets on the other end. This is when they realize they should've been making noise in town long before their doors were officially opened. Once consumers know you're there, your name is automatically added to their list of shopping options, regardless of whether you've been able to convince them to shop with you or not. Your brand is designed to do that kind of heavy lifting, but only you can get your customers excited about getting to know that brand. Without marketing before your launch, you're just giving yourself more work during a time when the less you have to worry about doing, the better. Putting in the effort to communicate the value you plan to offer to any potential and existing customers, partners, clients, and so forth is almost non-negotiable if you want your business to be successful.

I had studied graphic design and could create a webpage at practically no cost. But as I began to think it through, Facebook was by far the better option for marketing and customer development. Social media has become this unbelievably vast and free marketplace where people from all over the world can share their ideas and creations on a global scale with little to no money or time. Knowing this, I chose Facebook as the initial platform for Ansell Dresses. I'd already had a personal page. One day while I looked at my page and all the friends I had from back home in Uganda, I thought about how easy it was to keep in touch with anybody I'd met. From cousins and classmates to friends I'd made over time, these were the people I had unfettered access to. Even better, there was a built-in mechanism for sharing information about my store from contact to contact. This made me think of how easy it would be to sell my dresses to these same contacts, even if I was living in a different country. Instantaneously, word could travel about my store as people linked and shared. Right away, I set up a page for Ansell Dresses and made the plan to advertise the dresses for sale through there. People would post pictures of their events and social activities, and they'd be wearing my dresses. People would "like" their pictures, post comments, and share when they bought them. I realized Facebook was not only the most cost-effective platform for marketing Ansell Dresses but also the most efficient. It was literally built to do exactly what I needed better than any other source I could develop.

Using my personal page, I searched through my existing friends and friends of friends to find women who matched the characteristics that defined my brand. Women with effortless style and undeniable confidence who would be looking for exactly what I had to offer. Socially active young professionals were key. These were the women searching the most for my styles and sharing them often with others. I'd just look at the pictures posted on their profiles, and if I liked the way they were dressed, I'd friend them and introduce myself. I'd let them know I was living in the US, and that I could provide them with quality dresses they probably would love to buy. I would also tell them I had access to plenty of other things in the States if they ever wanted to have me purchase and ship them to wherever they were. I marketed myself like a personal shopper. I was there to help them with their shopping needs in the US, and they could count on me to be readily available and easy to contact. It was important I clearly communicated my purpose for contacting them. I needed to make them feel comfortable with the idea of paying me to solve a problem in their lives. A problem they didn't realize they had until I pointed it out. With all my messages sent, these women became potential clients. If none accepted my requests or responded, I would be in no worse condition than where I started. But if even one person responded, my chances of selling were pushed even further.

If you are starting a side hustle or a business of your own, using social media as a platform to carry out your marketing strategy is not at all a requirement. Although you'd be giving up a pretty fantastic tool, there are plenty of other ways to market your brand without creating your own social media page the way I did. Traditional advertisements through billboards, magazines, and TV commercials have always been an excellent example of marketing. However, these kinds of marketing tools often cost a lot of money that newly launched businesses will not have on hand, which is the exact reason why I chose social media as my platform for marketing Ansell Dresses. I thoughtfully considered whether the return on investment would be worth the expense. A commercial may reach 10,000 people but only yield 10 customers who purchase $50 each. If you've paid $1k for that commercial it means you spent $100 per customer and lost $50 on each. Those same customers reached through a free social media platform would put $500 into your pocket. At the end of the day, you have to do what makes sense for your business. A young entrepreneur with a lemonade stand in the middle of a suburban cul-de-sac in Pennsylvania will not buy a nationally circulated TV commercial to sell their product. They're going to tell their neighbors and friends themselves – knocking on doors and waving to any cars and people that pass them by – marketing solely through word of mouth. If your customer base is the other parents at your child's school, you might use the same route or combine that with fliers, announcements, or newsletters. In your case, think deeply about how you want people to find out about your business, about whether this concept will actually sway them to shop with you and think hard about whether it will be cost-efficient.

When it comes to marketing, I find many first-time business owners make mistakes and poor decisions because they miss the most basic point. Marketing inevitably makes you money. Getting word out about your company is great, but only if it leads to revenue. It's wonderful to have a million "likes" on Facebook, but at some point, those "likes" need to be converted to sales. New entrepreneurs often confuse how well their business is doing with how much they are being recognized. It's not as simple as reaching as many people as you can. You have to reach the people who are likely to take the next step of engaging with your company through their purchases. Following that, there needs to be a way to actually measure how effective a marketing strategy is. And the more able you are to tie customers to the method used, the better your understanding of which marketing initiatives are most worth it. Rough estimates, such as comparing the number of "likes" to actual sales, for instance, is a good starting point. But the more sophisticated and precise you can be in determining how your sales are coming in and where from on an ongoing basis, the more likely you'll be to continue marketing in a way that keeps those sales high.

## Budgeting

Having a positive money mindset is of utmost importance if you want to attract more money into your life. To be honest, I love money. I always have. To be even more honest, I'm the type of person who says I'm 50/50 on the subject of whether money buys happiness. I wouldn't call myself greedy, but I do have a taste for the finer things in life. If for any reason I found myself down and out, I'd rather be crying in a Bentley than drying my eyes on a bicycle. Money is so much more than just colored paper you work for. It enables survival, shows status, and commands respect. I respect money. It most importantly provides the freedom we need to do the things in life we want. Of course, money can't bring us everything. We all know money can't buy us love, more breath in our lungs, or turn back the hands of time. But aside from those, most other things have a definite price. The truth is, you can have anything you want in this world as long as you're not too lazy to go out and get it. And when you have money, you'll find you can make it work for you, so you don't have to do as much. There's another quote from *Rich Dad, Poor Dad* that fits well here. It reads, "By not fully understanding money, the vast majority of people allow its awesome power to control them." Money can do so many things for our lives, but only if we're the ones in control. Being in control starts with budgeting.

Learning how to budget your money is such an important financial skill for anyone to have, whether you want to own your own business or not. If you have no idea how your money is being spent, most likely it's spending you. Having a budget and monitoring it closely allows you to track where every dollar is going, helping you to spend and save more effectively for the things you may want now and in the future. I'm the kind of person that likes to track my money down to the hour. If I say I want to make $1 million in the year with my business, then I break it down. *By the end of the year, I want to make this, so every month, I need to be making that, and each day has to be such and such amount, so every hour I have to be making…* That's just my train of thought. With this type of reverse profit budgeting, if $1 million is the number, I know every hour I'm not doing something to develop my businesses, I'm losing $114. This helps me remain on track to increase my earnings goals as I monitor what's coming in. Most importantly, it ensures I'm not spending money I don't have as I keep track of what's going out. When it comes to your business, an accurate account of expenses is critical information.

Through the years, I developed a system for cost analysis and formatted it into a streamlined business plan template. For new entrepreneurs or first time side hustlers, it's a terrific tool to guide you through the process of uncovering all costs and expenses you wouldn't otherwise consider. I developed mine because when I searched for something comparable, everything I found required far more information than was actually needed. If you are not pitching to gain venture capital or pleading for a loan, you'll need something simple to help you take the steps toward startup.

In the case of Ansell Dresses, I began with what I believed would be my most costly obstacle – shipping. If my plans were to buy dresses in the US to be sold in Uganda, I needed to know from the beginning how much it would cost for me to get them there. I'd already dealt with situations in the past where I couldn't even start a side hustle because it would cost too much for the operations – namely my attempt at selling Egyptian towels. To make sure I was going to reach my profit goal of $5k a month, I needed to know exactly what the costs would be. Through my research I began asking myself critical questions and comparing options. Would I pay-per-pound, or were there flat-rate boxes I could use for shipping? If there were flat rate boxes, what were their sizes, and which ones should I purchase? If I had to pay-per-pound, how many garments could I possibly ship without breaking the bank? Was there insurance involved in case my items were lost or damaged? What was the cost of insurance compared to the cost of potential products I would be shipping? There were also figures on customs, duty, and tax calculation on imported goods that needed to be considered. How many buyers would I need to cover the costs of their orders along with the transport to get it to them? Once I had these numbers, I started to look at the dollar/shilling exchange rates to make sure I didn't incorrectly price the dresses for purchase in Uganda. If I underpriced, I obviously wouldn't make much money. If I overpriced, I ran the risk of losing customers I didn't have yet.

Next to consider was the cost of potential product loss. Because I'd lived in Uganda, I knew not every package reached its destination with all of its contents. It's not uncommon for packages to be opened and for each person who handles them to help themselves. Although I had trustworthy people on the receiving end, my dresses would pass through many intermediaries I did not know. There was a really good chance not all of them would get there. I would be able to estimate the costs for product losses, but I wouldn't be able to accurately predict or calculate the cost of losing a customer because they didn't receive what they expected. That loss was exponential. I stood to lose all current sales, then all sales to the people that particular customer would have brought to the store had they been satisfied, and their future purchases. To the best of my ability, I estimated potential costs for these losses, and began to think about other logistical problems that would impact customer satisfaction. When I finished my research on shipping, I had a strong understanding of how to proceed. From there, I turned my attention to products and suppliers.

I looked up the average prices of dresses I was looking to buy and sell – brand new, top-quality, plus-size garments with an undeniable American style for any occasion. That search led me to leading department stores where I could buy these kinds of dresses affordably, like Macy's and JCPenney. Further research revealed the price ranges most consumers would agree to pay. With those, I'd estimate how much money I'd need on hand to buy the initial inventory. Having the estimated prices for shipping and merchandise, among other costs, I resolved that if I wanted to turn a profit and validate my idea, then I couldn't spend more than $20 on any one dress. If I spent more than $20, I risked compromising my profit margins and losing money. Had I not done my research beforehand, this could've easily happened.

Lastly, I had to decide how I would pay the upfront costs of the dresses and their delivery. Ansell Dresses was the first business I'd be starting where there would be upfront costs to consider. All of my other ventures generally required no money to start because they were service-oriented, and I was the one providing the labor. If anything did require money, the amount was minimal, and I would typically use whatever I was making from current projects to fund the idea. However, I'd just moved to the US, so I presently had no source of income. My cake business in Cairo had been very profitable, but before leaving, I'd funneled those profits into a house I was building in Uganda. Though in time that property would be even more valuable, it was not yet a source of revenue. Most entrepreneurship methods instruct potential business owners to spend money upfront in order to make it. They also stress that businesses only work when the entrepreneur is 'all in,' meaning they now have something to lose, possibly everything. In my opinion, this is the wrong approach as it creates the opposite result of what's intended. In my experience, those who pay to start a business are less successful.

The minute you put money into a potential business, you are working at a loss. Being in the red from the beginning does something to the way you think. Instead of seeing your business venture as a helpful way to gain more than what you have, you see it as something that's already set you back. Your business then becomes an entity which you have to recuperate from instead of one to nurture and build. With this outlook comes an overwhelming fear of failure, breeding irrational decision-making and improper strategizing. This fear could cause you to put more time, money, and effort into things that, out of desperation seem lucrative, but would never pay off. It might also prevent you from seeing clearly, causing you to quit or scale back your efforts too quickly. These emotional rather than intellectual decisions often bring costly mistakes. In light of these mistakes, you'll need to be able to walk away when things are no longer working. However, if you've already put in money, walking away can seem nearly impossible. The only time I put money into a business is after I've made money from that business. And even then, I only put money where it will unquestionably help grow the business to earn more.

Then there's the business development strategy that involves starting a company or creating a product first, then seeking money from investors, venture capitalists, grants, loans or some other source afterward to help fund it. This has never appealed to me. Maybe I'm too much of a control freak, but I don't really believe in starting a business you need to get funding for. Once you accept money, you must answer to the source. And I'm simply not built to operate that way. I don't like having to answer to someone else. It's literally the reason why I'm self-employed – the reason why I'm an entrepreneur – I don't like being told what to do. I didn't even like taking my own husband's money to fund my ideas. Anytime you take someone's money, even if you're using it to do what you want, you still have some level of obligation to answer to them. You will have to do your best to please them because it's their money you're using. Whether it's a silent partner or a gift, there are always strings attached even with a promise of zero involvement. There will always be an expectation in there somewhere.

Starting a business is stressful by itself, and we all have our own visions of the way things will go once they get off the ground. But if you're taking someone else's money into your account, then you have to take their perspective into account. If they see things differently, that's just added stress for you. Now you'll have to fight twice as hard to accomplish your goal. On the one hand, you'll be building your business. On the other hand, you'll be working hard at convincing your sponsor to come around to your way of thinking each time you make a decision. And if they expect something from your business, like a royalty, a repayment, or percentage of the profits, they take it first, and you take what's remaining. That never sounded like an agreeable way of operating to me. You and your business are best when you are beholden to no one. So I've always been adamant that if I have some business idea I think would do well but it requires money I don't have to start, I just hold off until I do. However, with Ansell Dresses, I wasn't willing to hold off because it wasn't like the startup costs were going to be thousands of dollars. In the end, I decided to use my credit card to buy and ship the first handful of dresses. $750 would be my spending limit and I would have until the bill came due in one month to sell the dresses and pay the charge.

## Scheduling

While thinking of how I would launch, grow, and maintain the business, my greatest consideration was time. Setting aside time where you'll only be focused on the creation and cultivation of your business is important for you to keep yourself from becoming overwhelmed. There's nothing wrong with making things up as you go along. We all want freedom; it's the reason why we're starting our own businesses. But being the boss takes the kind of time and energy you're better off organizing before attempting to use it. Even if I wouldn't have a physical store to go to or hours to log, I still needed to carve out time in my schedule for when

I would run the business. I had always been adept and skilled at managing my time and was very good at using just about every hour of the day for something productive. Before moving to the US, I had a predictable life. Time was mine to control and easy to arrange. At that point, I had two toddlers under the age of two years old, I'd just moved to a new country I still had to learn about, my husband was working, and we only had one car to share. Whatever schedule I came up with had to be airtight. Just as important to examine was the value of my time, something many newer entrepreneurs fail to consider or calculate.

Your time has value. And the amount of time you truly have available will have a direct impact on your profit margin. I understand that every hour I spend on a business has a corresponding dollar amount. I needed to make sure the time I would put in would be worth what I would earn for my efforts. For example, if I spend eighty hours a week on a business and after a month my profit is $2k, it means I've made roughly $6.25 per hour. That's less than minimum wage, and therefore not worth my time or energy to continue. Without doing that calculation, though, it is easy to overlook. Even worse, people think, "That's ok, I love doing it. In time it will pick up, and I'll earn more." These statements mean nothing when you have goals to reach. I've coached several women who have wanted to start side hustles from their hobbies. Knitting is one of the top choices. They choose this as a potential business opportunity because they love doing it. Everyone assumes since they'll have to spend so many hours immersed in the work to start and grow their business, they better really love what they're doing. But a successful business is run by your head, not your heart. Hobbies are not businesses. Businesses are something you do for money. Hobbies are something you do for free. When you do the math you find that the hours and hours you enjoyably spend knitting that blanket, scarf, or hat you sell will earn you roughly $1.13 per hour. At that rate, if your goal is to make $200 a month, you're right on track. But if you were looking to supplement or even replace your income, you need to go in a different direction. I knew this and factored it in as I carved out time to launch Ansell Dresses.

I decided that every day from 12 p.m.-2 p.m. I would put my kids down for their nap and use the time while they were asleep to take pictures of whatever dresses I'd be selling. Each night at 7 p.m. when I'd put my children to bed, I planned to use a couple of hours to edit and review the pictures before I posted them to the Ansell Dresses Facebook page. After this, I'd have time to myself for relaxing, cleaning up, or whatever I would need to do to get a jumpstart on the next day. Between 9:30 p.m. and 10:30 p.m., I'd post the final pictures to the Facebook page. With the time difference, everyone with eyes on the page would see the new posts at around 5 a.m. Ugandan time. This was perfect because then my posts would be one of the first things people saw as they started their day. Even if it was only a quick glance while they checked their page after waking up, I hoped it would put Ansell Dresses on their minds first thing in the morning while they got dressed and ready for work. I also hoped people would surf social media as they killed time on their way to work or while stealing quick breaks when they got there. I figured they might say something like, "Oh yeah, I remember I saw those new dresses posted this morning, let me go back and take another look." From there, they might show their coworkers, talk about upcoming social events, and compare what they were going to wear. A new morning post every day would routinely put my dresses into the middle of those conversations. Even pushing shoppers to keep an eye out on the page until they found the dress they needed for whatever event they had coming up. Posting has been extremely important for my sales, and since I've seen the positive impact it's had from the beginning, I've never done anything differently.

Once my social media page was up and running, and I'd carved out time for maintaining it, I called my sister back home in Uganda. I needed someone to receive the packages of merchandise I sent to deliver the orders to each of my clients. Once my sister agreed, and she was ready to receive the orders, all that was left for me to do was execute.

## Execution

One of the biggest reasons most businesses never get started is simply because their potential founders never start them. Some hold on to their ideas and sit on them, saying to themselves, "Wow! That's such a great idea," but never do anything to manifest them. There are even more times when another person executes their same idea, and the person who did nothing is left saying, "I thought of that first!" Sadly, by the time they say this, that sentiment means nothing at all. Who's to say you had the idea to do something when you have nothing to show for it? Other potential founders get caught up in their research phase, afraid to move forward even when what they've found tells them their plan could be a success. That's called analysis-paralysis. You spend so much time worrying, questioning, planning, and thinking you never really do anything at all. With this mindset, the business you've built in your mind can only be run there and nowhere else. Meticulous and obsessive research is key, but once that's done, acting has to follow. Both of these instances of non-action are totally governed by fear and self-limiting beliefs. Feelings you hold about yourself or your situation that trick you into thinking you could never be successful. But to be successful, you must first try. You might fail, but it will never be the end of the world, just the start of a newer, more refined plan. Once you've fallen, if you do, then you get back up again. The first step of your new plan would be to learn from the mistakes of your past.

Of course, there were plenty of things I wasn't sure of when it came to starting Ansell Dresses, but I didn't let that stop me from seeing it to fruition. I assumed, but wasn't 100% sure people would buy from me. I wasn't even sure if people were going to accept my friend requests or read the messages I sent. I wasn't sure if the dresses I sent would get to Kampala without any issues, and I had no idea of how many dresses I would actually sell, even though I projected it would be all of them. But spending most of my life living the way I did, and starting all my side hustles, meant when it came time to launch Ansell Dresses, there was no hesitation. The launch wasn't something big and scary because I had a plan I could follow and a goal I was confident I'd meet. All I had to do was get up and do the things I knew needed to be done. Anything I wasn't sure of up to that point was out of my hands until further notice.

I am, by nature, and as most other entrepreneurs are, a risk-taker. And I love it. As much as I advocate for careful and meticulous research, it will still be a leap of faith when it's time to finally pull the trigger and take action, no matter how much you know and believe. The only way you can see if something works is if you try to make it work. Because I know this, I never hesitate to try new things or risk failure. To me it makes more sense to try and fail than to hope and never try. Unfortunately, being a risk-taker is not a very common trait. People are naturally averse to risk, and many can't get off the ground with a business venture or even a small side hustle because of it. Most people prefer to play it safe, protect their assets, and live their lives realistically, according to what's socially acceptable or normal. Why risk the unknown when you can survive on the familiar? It's a way of life many people choose. And there's absolutely nothing wrong with living your life this way, as long as you don't want to win big. Because the bigger the risk, the bigger the reward. So if you want more, you'll have to do more, knowing deep down if things don't work out, you stand to lose more than you're comfortable with. Knowledge of this should only push you to work even harder, stir you to create a seemingly bulletproof plan, and do whatever it takes to ensure you don't lose. A true entrepreneur knows there will be problems, setbacks, barriers, and many risks, but they never allow these to be reasons they quit before beginning. Take a risk, and you may improve your situation beyond what you expected. Avoid the risk, and your situation will stay the same.

If you have an aversion to taking risks but want to get over it, once again I suggest starting as small as you can. Buy a lottery ticket. Bet on yourself to lose the weight you gained with your last pregnancy. Vow to donate $100 to charity if you don't lose weight at the specified time. Attempt to convince your friends to try a new bar or restaurant with you. Ask the guy you've been crushing on for months on a date. Find something in your life you would normally shy away from, something you fear might end badly, and face it head-on. If you want to come up with a plan beforehand, even better, but make sure you actually do what you've been afraid of. Because you never know how it will turn out until it finally does, and only you can make that happen.

With my business plan finalized, I waited for the weekend to go shopping. With our two kids in the stroller, my husband and I went to the mall. I already knew what my budget was for each dress, so anything over $20 I quickly flipped past. Since it was nearing the end of the summer, most of the dresses were on sale anyway, so I had a good selection to choose from. From the time I'd spent on Facebook looking at pictures of potential customers, I'd gotten a sense of their styles and tastes. Keeping these in mind as I shopped, I knew exactly what to look for. On Saturday, we went to one mall, and on Sunday, we went to another. I was sure to take advantage of all the stores available to me. On Monday, while the kids napped, I took pictures just as I'd planned. I made sure I put them up on hangers against the back of the door to show the dresses off and keep the shots looking clean and professional. Then I packed the dresses into boxes. Once the kids woke up from their naps, I got us ready, we got in the car and drove straight to the shipping center. With that shipment, which was about $200, I'd spent about $700 altogether in startup costs.

While the boxes were in transit, I went back to Facebook and started marketing as my business's life depended on it. There was no way I would be able to sell more than two dresses if people in Uganda didn't know that I was selling them. So I kept friending more people, messaging them from my personal page, and introducing myself. I would let them know who I was, where I was, and that I could get access to whatever they wanted. I told them I was open to special orders if they needed, and that I already had dresses that would be arriving in Kampala shortly. By the time the dresses arrived, I'd sold every single one of them. My new clients were all lining up to receive their orders with plenty of others behind them, asking if they could order too. I'd spent an average of $17 per dress with this first shipment, and I'd sold each for $100. After expenses, I'd made nearly $2,700. And as soon as my sister sent me the money, I put every last penny right back into the business, giving me the funds I needed to buy even more dresses and continue growing to meet my goal. That first shipment was validation that not only the idea but the business model would work. I was on the right track and would continue doing what I was already doing – following a solid plan I knew was effective.

## When It Comes To Growth, Let Your Customers Lead The Way

I generally believe you should only start a business when you have an achievable goal that's small enough to reach. Within three months, the sales from Ansell Dresses had outgrown my original goal. Prior to launch, my hope was to make $5k a month. By the fourth month, I was making closer to $8k. If things continued, I'd be on track to make closer to $100k in my first year. But I knew not to get too ahead of myself. I'd made consistent profits during that time, but I was cautiously optimistic I had a winning strategy. The money reflected that. But I also knew this was a new venture, and I could already see potential issues that would prevent me from scaling. It usually takes about six months for any new business to get off the ground. During that first six months to one year of operating your business, you should only focus on making money. The amount of money you're making is what proves your concept. If the amount is less than the target or goal and a simple shift in strategy doesn't change that, it's not worth it to continue. If the amount consistently exceeds the target, it makes sense to think about what next steps could set you on the path to the next level. Now that you know your idea works, you might want to move quickly into what's next, but you should take your time figuring that out. In the first six months to a year, while the processes are being sorted out and customers are being established, revenue and expenses could waver, impacting profit. You have to give things time to settle before you try to set a newer, bigger goal. You need to pause, and stop growing to take a closer look at what you've been doing, how you've been doing it, and how much money you've been able to keep from doing those things. With that information, you need to put a plan into place, one with all new processes and procedures that fit what you're trying to do with the business. At this point, you would've spent enough time learning exactly what's worked, what hasn't, and what could be improved upon in the long run. Without a plan, you run the risk of growing too fast, selling out too often, or compromising the quality or service your customers have come to know.

Some people don't like to admit it, but the customer really is always right. The customer is the part of your business that actively brings you the money you're looking for. Why wouldn't you listen to what they have to say? Even if they are not always accurate, their voices are important. Your customers can spot the holes in your business quicker than you can distract them with the bright spots you want them to focus on. They will be brutally honest with you about what they think you're missing because whatever you fall short on directly affects their own experience. The fact remains – the success of your business depends on the happiness of your customers. If your customers are not happy, then they're not your customers. As the lifeblood of your business, the people who choose to spend their money with you are special and deserve your undivided attention and complete consideration as you grow what you've built.

As Ansell Dresses grew, the first thing I needed to re-evaluate was the shipping. Not only were the costs exorbitant, which increased my prices and cut into my profit margin, but the shipments were taking an extremely long time to be delivered. I needed to figure out an alternative plan of action. It reached a point where I was sending so many boxes each week, I looked into buying a plane ticket to Uganda. Thinking back to my cell phone side hustle in Egypt, I considered flying with the dresses myself, and paying the luggage fees at the airport instead of the separate shipping I was already paying an arm and a leg for. I crunched the numbers and found that even if I brought along my two kids, the tickets would cost almost the same. Maybe even a little bit cheaper than what I was already paying for shipping. An added benefit of flying with the dresses was the ability it gave me to meet my clients face-to-face and see how things were really going. Having my feet and eyes on the ground, I could find out what my clients really liked and gain a better understanding of the current market in Uganda. So, I purchased the tickets, three seats for my kids and me, and we flew to Kampala with the dresses in tow. Before we left, I made sure I continued marketing, letting my clients know I'd be in the city with the dresses very soon. I even sent messages to some celebrities, thinking sooner or later I would capture the attention of at least one. I didn't really get any responses to those, it didn't hurt to try. I was mostly trying to push special orders. My special order customers were starting to emerge and I realized what great potential there was in building that facet of my business. Luxury brands like Chanel, Gucci, Prada, Louis Vuitton, and Yves St. Laurent were difficult to get in Uganda, but there were people with money who wanted them. If I could convince people to make special orders with me before I got there, then when I landed in Kampala with the $100 perfume or $200 pair of shoes the client specially ordered, I'd have the opportunity to sell them one of the 300 dresses I had with me. It was my, "Have popcorn, need a candle too?" strategy reborn in high fashion.

When I landed and set up shop in the house I'd invested in building, it was a huge eye-opener. I noticed there were many customers we were delivering to, but there were also people who lived close by and didn't mind coming to my house to pick up what they ordered. I'd told my customers I'd be bringing a large selection of dresses in 60-70 pound bags with me. They were excited to look through everything else we had and prepared to buy what they liked on site. Because I'd made an effort to communicate this ahead of time, most of the people actually did end up coming. There was one point where two women spent nearly $2k each with me barely doing anything besides showing them what I'd brought. It ended up being a huge success. My being there, having a location, and offering options people could see and touch made the difference. Customers bought much more than they typically did online, and my initial instinct about selling only one dress of each style clearly drove sales up even more. Customers had a limited time to act, and that incentive to buy was driven by the sense that *now* was their chance. Seeing all that take place solidified a new routine for me to visit Uganda at least once every two to three months delivering special orders, bringing dresses, holding house sales, and earning, what was for me at that time, a fortune. Because not only did I learn more by going, but I earned more. That wasn't something I was about to give up.

By the time I'd made my first trip to Uganda for Ansell Dresses, I wasn't doing anything differently than what I'd done on day one. I was still going to the malls on weekends and shopping with my kids in their strollers. I'd added some evenings to my shopping schedules, but I was still taking pictures while my kids napped, posting to the Facebook page every single day at the same exact time, and using the same pricing methods. I wasn't doing much extra, yet my business was growing exponentially. From the beginning, I focused on being consistent and that paid off. My clients had become fully engaged to the point they were loyal followers of Ansell Dresses. And everyone around them was beginning to notice. Soon people I hadn't even reached out to directly were finding out about us and quickly buying out everything I put up on the site. In no time at all, we could no longer keep up with the deliveries. Taking this as a sign it was time to set up a storefront, I jumped in headfirst. It was an exciting experience, but unfortunately, very short-lived.

There are two ways to learn from experience. The first is by doing everything right. The second is by doing everything wrong. When you're an entrepreneur you do both. I'd rented a spot in downtown Kampala, and within a month, realized it was the biggest mistake I could've made. I chose a spot in the middle of the central shopping district, thinking it would bring even more customers. There was a high amount of foot traffic in the area, and there would always be people there shopping and casually walking by. This would give them the perfect opportunity to look into our windows and see what we had. By that logic, the place should have been perfect. But it turned out to be the reason why it didn't work. The same kind of people I'd hoped to influence with our displays were the kind of shoppers who didn't walk through the shopping district to spend money. Most of the people it attracted were there to window shop. They were the kind of people who went for strolls through the area to stretch their legs and take in the sights. Not only were they not there to shop, but they really couldn't afford what we were selling. They were aspirational rather than actual customers. Our presence in the shopping district and subsequent exposure to hundreds of more people did nothing to change this. Even more concerning, and surprising, was the impact it had on our existing clientele. They flat out weren't coming to the store. They were the kinds of people who had their own cars and worked in the city but lived on the outskirts, and the traffic to get to where Ansell Dresses was located from there was terrible. Clients weren't willing to sit in traffic all day, so they'd ask if we could still make deliveries even though I was already paying rent for the store. Now I had the added cost of rent with no reduction in delivery costs. And without a significant increase in sales at the store, expenses were hardly being covered. We were losing money. So, shortly after opening our doors, I closed the location. But even though we were closed, I still kept my eyes open for a new place to move. From that experience, I learned what would work and understood what should be done. We did need a storefront, because the inventory was significant and we could not sustain a distribution system that relied on deliveries. In addition, flying to Uganda for a sales event every two to three months was no longer often enough. There were enough customers, demands for clothing, and special order items that I was in danger of losing clients if they had to wait. I needed to find a place that was on the outskirts with a lot of parking and out of the way of traffic for my existing clients because they were the ones who'd been there from the beginning. They were the foundation of Ansell Dresses. I trusted that if I catered to them, I'd be making the right decision.

In no time at all, I found a new location that was perfect. However, it was evident it might present some challenges for us moving forward. It had everything we needed. The retail center would attract buying customers in addition to window shoppers. The store would be located in a mall, so there was no worry about parking. I could tell that in the future I would get plenty of new clients. The risky part was the fact that if I wanted to secure the spot, I had to move in right away. At the time, the mall was still under construction. My clients would literally have to walk through a construction zone to buy their dresses. I knew they were engaged, but I didn't have total confidence this would be something they'd tolerate. And if I was going to be able to afford the expense of a storefront, I would need the expenses of deliveries to be offset. This was a risk. It could go in the same direction as the first storefront. And I didn't have time for due diligence or research but I had learned from my last attempt at securing a storefront. I adjusted, and had never been one to back down in the face of a risk. So, I made the investment anyway. I put the deposit down on the space and Ansell Dresses opened its doors in August of 2013. If I was wrong, I would learn and pivot again. Interestingly enough, all of our existing clients came out and shopped with us almost immediately. They loved not having to wait for shipping or sit in traffic. In fact, they cared about removing these inconveniences so much, they gladly walked underneath ladders and through giant sheets of plastic to buy their dresses out of my store. Before the end of that first year of business, Ansell Dresses had made $100k in profits.

From one idea born out of frustration to a Facebook page, then an abandoned storefront to a beautiful location where we planned to be for years to come, all with six-figure profits within the first year. This journey was an amazing sight to see. When I realized the store had made that much money, I felt incredible. Like I'd made it. I'd proven to myself I could start a business even in the most cutthroat of places. I recognized I had a gift for building upon what I already knew to create something I'd never seen before. Even though I hadn't been living in the US for that long, I was able to figure my way around things. I applied the same general business principles I'd been using most of my life to start a business that was making so much money. It was monumental. It really cemented my belief that the way I created and grew businesses was something anyone could do, anywhere in the world. It made me feel secure to know that because I could do that, I'd probably never go hungry again. It made me think of what other amazing things I could possibly accomplish. And how did I respond to this incredible accomplishment and milestone? I did what I always had. I kept moving forward. Right then and there, I decided. By the time I turned 25, I was going to be a millionaire.

# CHAPTER 7

# Trouble In Paradise

## A lesson on facing hardships

I don't think I've had another moment in my life that felt as exhilarating as that first time I made six figures with Ansell Dresses. Up until that point, I'd never felt more proud of myself for what I'd been able to accomplish. Soon after reaching this milestone, I'd received a text message from my brother-in-law. It was one of hundreds of mundane text messages he and I have exchanged throughout the years, but this one I remember distinctly. He'd lived in New York at the time and wanted to check in on all of us in Pittsburgh. He asked about work, the kids, and some general questions about how we were adjusting. I don't remember having one bad thing to say. I thought to myself, everything is perfect. I had healthy children, a loving husband, our half a million-dollar home, my successful businesses, and several budding investments. Between the time I'd entered the country up to when I was texting him on the other side of $100k in profits, I'd been able to do so many amazing things in my life and career. Where

I'd come from and what I'd accomplished felt immense, and I felt a rush of lightness and energy. At that moment I couldn't have been happier. Which is kind of ironic considering the fact that the entire year and a half leading up to that moment, I'd been almost completely unhappy.

A large part of entrepreneurship involves taking big risks and banking on everything you planned to work out perfectly. However, when no one on the face of this Earth can plan for each present moment of their lives, it becomes reasonable for anyone uncomfortable with this level of uncertainty to decide against betting on themselves. Whether you're launching a brand new product the market has never seen, or you're getting down on one knee to propose to the one you love, there's always room for things to go wrong. No matter how definite you are about something or how perfectly you believe it will turn out, there is still so much outside of your control. Building and growing a business is hard work, and being a full-time entrepreneur is definitely not for the faint of heart. When it comes to all forms of goal-setting unrelated to entrepreneurship, the same idea stands. Things don't always go according to plan. In the world of entrepreneurship, your product could be deemed defective and cause a lawsuit that ruins the trust of your brand, or your expensive commercial doesn't get played, and you miss out on the chance to reach the audience that could've saved you from bankruptcy. In the world of your personal life, the stakes often seem so much higher. What if you decide to go back to college after you've been out of school for 30 years, only to fail every class, put yourself in deeper debt, and miss out on the degree you've been waiting almost your entire life to receive?

There are plenty of things that can go right as we journey toward our goals, but it's almost inevitable that some things go the exact opposite. But who's to say any of those *bad* outcomes can't be for our benefit?

The way I've told you the story of Ansell Dresses sounds very neat and clean. This is because I've told it through the lens of a business plan or development strategy. I pointed out the steps I took and gave you insight into the mind of an entrepreneur. But what I did not share was all of the things that occurred in my personal life along with those analytical decisions and careful actions I was making as a businesswoman. The truth is, any woman in business, any mother starting a side hustle, any person who is both a spouse and an entrepreneur has to work through more than just a solid business plan as they launch and grow a business. They juggle life and career, constantly searching for balance, improvising when things don't go as planned, and unfortunately, having to settle at times. I was certainly no exception. This is the part of the Ansell Dresses story where I give you a glimpse into all of those things happening behind the scenes while I drove to hit that first-year milestone.

## Nothing Ever Happens Exactly The Way You Think It Will

While I was scaling Ansell Dresses to what it is today, I was going through *a lot*. Looking back, the challenges began when my husband decided to move back to his hometown before we left Egypt. Prior to our arrival in the US, I'd moved from Uganda to London, then Hurghada, and finally Cairo, slipping into each culture, figuring out how to live and work. Each place was drastically different from the other, but it was never difficult for me to adjust. Whatever place I found myself in very quickly felt like home, and I was making it work for me. My move to the US was completely different. It was a struggle. The truth of the matter was, I'd never even wanted to move when we did back in 2012. This was mostly because I saw our move to the US as something that would happen further down the road, rather than as soon as it did. When we were first married, our plan was to have our family right away. My husband was established in his career, and there were terrific professional opportunities for him in dozens of places around the world. Every three to four years, he would have a choice of a new location to work. Ideally, we would have four children in the time he was taking advantage of these opportunities so that when they were school-aged, we'd settle in the US and raise them there. I saw the time we had before that point as time we were free to move and live where we wanted. This was important to me. I knew what I'd be giving when I had children – my time, energy, body, and own needs. And I was ready to provide all of those things and more. I just wanted to do it in a way that made sense for me. Moving to the US was settling, and I wasn't ready to do that just yet. Knowing it was only a matter of time before I would be pregnant again made me a little annoyed since I'd have my health, changing babies, and chasing toddlers to think about while I worked to get acclimated. But then I would get even more annoyed when I thought about the fact that my husband had other options to choose from when it came to where we were going to move during that time.

I remember two places in particular that I thought would've been better for all of us, but with him dead set on moving back right then, I felt like we were going to be missing out. One of the positions was in Abu Dhabi. That was a time when the market in the United Arab Emirates was booming, and I had multiple business ideas I was sure would've easily taken off. Another offer was in Paris, which was such a beautiful, historic city and connected to everything. The idea of living there for several years was exciting to me. And with either of these choices, he would've had the chance to make even more money than he could in the States, but none of that happened. It was his work, so it was his decision. Seeing my husband happy was important to me, but when he chose Pittsburgh, Pennsylvania, deep down I was kind of salty. I'd wanted so badly for him to consider the options. I wanted to create solutions that would give us both exactly what we wanted and needed. I wanted to be heard but didn't have the words to express it. I knew his happiness was coming at the expense of my own.

I was an independent person in a reluctantly dependent position. I wasn't even certain I was entirely justified in feeling what I was feeling. *I* was now a *we*, and *we* agreed this was the right move for us. When I was forced to leave London before I was ready, I was resentful. But I made the best of it, turning my attention to the possibilities and finding reasons to be optimistic. It was the same with my move to the US. By the time I arrived, I was focused on all of the good things that could be. But I carried a tiny bit of resentment with me, like a little pebble in my shoe. From time to time, I'd feel that little resentment pebble, especially when I was dealing with something difficult. Regardless of whether it was rational or not, I would be confronted with a problem or hit a huge barrier and think, on some level, this would not be an issue if my life had taken a different direction.

When it came to Ansell Dresses, I remember the first package we sent took *forever* to get to Uganda. It was several weeks more than what it should have taken. As time went on, the shipping became more and more expensive. And not just from the weight of the merchandise, but because of where the containers were having to travel. I was never naive to the corruption issues in some governments, and I understood that my home country had its fair share. I just thought that if I used reputable shipping companies, I'd be able to minimize the risks involved. It turns out, I was completely wrong. For the first three months I was shipping to Uganda, it was really challenging sending the clothes because sometimes the packages would be held up in customs for no real reason. Most of the time, someone was holding it to make extra money for themselves. I could've paid $500 in taxes, but they would want me to pay an extra $1k directly to them just to release my stuff. Other times, the shipment could get stuck in a different place and we'd get robbed, like the time it was stopped in Mombasa. About a third of the dresses were missing once my sister was finally able to make the pickup. The extent of costs related to added fees, unexpected payments, and theft were much greater than what I could have anticipated in my projections. And trying to ship from the US, rather than other places in the world, was partly what made this problem more difficult to overcome. It was while I was grappling with this issue that I found out I was pregnant with our third child.

## Life Doesn't Come With A Set Of Instructions

There are two things I always knew I wanted: to own a business and to be a parent. I can't remember a time in my life when I wasn't sure that one day I would have both. And now that I did, I was trying to figure out how to make it all work. In my adult life, parenting has definitely been one of my greatest challenges. Because I never want my kids to lack, I work extremely hard to make sure they have everything they want and need. I always think back to what it felt like to lose the only home I'd ever known. All my stability had gone, and I was forced to create a new normal for myself without much support. That wasn't something I ever wanted for my kids. But doing that takes sacrifice. And sometimes that sacrifice looks like skipping out on extra rest to make sure I can get my work done before they get up from their naps. Or dragging them along with me to places they don't want to go so I can translate that time into money for all of us.

When we first moved to Pittsburgh, my son and daughter were under the age of two. Within a month, I'd started the dress store and it took off immediately. Now I had three babies, two human ones, and a business in its infancy. That's what I call my side hustles – baby businesses. They're so small but have the potential to grow rapidly. They also need so much care, patience, and supervision to survive – just like actual infants. With two of my real children needing just as much attention, and sometimes even more, it was a lot to handle. By then, I'd become an experienced caretaker and entrepreneur. I was used to working long hours and being responsible for myself and others at the same time. I was also used to juggling multiple demands and keeping a tight schedule to prevent things from falling through the cracks. But this was all happening at an altogether new level. I honestly had no idea how draining it could become.

I planned a schedule to manage and balance my time between my children and my business before I launched Ansell Dresses. But as the company ramped up, the demands increased. And while my baby business grew and needed more, so did my baby humans. Having a schedule is a wonderful and healthy thing for children, but it does not mean they will act predictably, dutifully, or stick to it. A little guy with an ear infection means no shopping trip. That means no dresses, and consequently, no business. That's not an option. A fussy little girl that won't go to sleep on time means no time for communications and posts. That means no sales, and in turn, no business. That can't happen. So, when something out of the ordinary happened, it didn't mean the business would fall by the wayside. It meant I'd have to find the time to do it all anyway. Sleeping, eating, showering – those were the things I had to sacrifice when either the needs of the business or the children bit into the time I set aside.

The more people in Uganda discovered Ansell Dresses, the more my schedule bent and shifted. To fulfill all the new orders, I'd started shopping upwards of five days a week. A sharp increase from the two I'd spent initially finding deals on weekends. My children routinely came with me. At first, I was focused and directed. I would shop as quickly as possible to alleviate the guilt I felt for dragging my kids along while I took care of the business' needs. I'd try to go straight to the stores where I found the best dresses, quickly get what I needed, and move on to something the kids would enjoy more. Sadly, this usually meant passing by an indoor children's play area. Every parent knows what happens when your child sees one of those! It's like they're put there with the intention of derailing every parent's to-do list. By my first or second shopping trip with my children, I knew it was useless to resist. I began to think of the play place and other kid-friendly activities at the malls as fair trade offs. If my kids had to be dragged around for three to four hours at a time so I could build Ansell Dresses, the least they could get in return was some solid play time. So that became our routine. Play for 30-45 minutes, then shop. Soon, they looked forward to going to the mall. From my perspective, starting at the play area was the perfect place for them to get rid of pent-up energy and tire themselves out before the long haul. Honestly, back then the trips could be exhausting for all of us. I never minded the extra rest.

Sometimes the kids would be asleep in their stroller while I walked miles and miles, up and down aisles, in and out of stores, pulling dresses on and off racks for hours and hours, day after day. There were so many nights where my arms, feet, back, and even my eyes (from looking at so many patterns) ached from the strain of it all. Sometimes, the kids would be awake just looking around, maybe playing with their toys or each other quietly. Other times, they would get bored and randomly start crying or fighting with each other. Then all of a sudden, I'm having to stop whatever I'm doing to soothe, distract, or calm them. Thankfully, these days were rare. However, knowing things are good most days doesn't make any difference when you're yelling at two toddlers in the middle of a mall and everything hurts. For a while, I was even feeling guilty.

It was as though I was robbing them of their childhood. I'd always wanted to raise my kids and run my businesses, but my plans for having them happen at different times fell through. I was growing them together now, but figuring out the best way to do that for the well-being of them both was a challenge I hadn't prepared for. I started to think about how they'd view our relationship as they got older. I didn't want them to resent me for keeping them quiet in department stores while other kids got to run outside screaming in parks. I cared so much about their happiness, but I never planned on discounting my own. Like every working mother, I wanted balance. Because there was no way to completely separate work from motherhood, I wanted to create some way to seamlessly integrate the two so both got the time and attention they deserved. The truth is, I didn't know what that looked like. Considering the way I grew up and the cultural norms of my childhood, this was a very new way for me to be thinking.

When I was growing up, my sister and I barely interacted with our parents. Although I've been in the US for almost as long as I have been a mother, I still sometimes find it strange to see kids and their parents playing together. When I was a child, adults and children rarely congregated in the same spaces. Those kinds of close relationships between parents and their children are so far from the cultural norm in Uganda and across the rest of the continent. Adults work and talk amongst themselves while children go to school and play with each other. They do most things separately. If they are together, the children do what the parents say, which is generally "Sit still, be quiet, and respect your elders." But the longer I've spent in American cities, the more I've seen how different the dynamics can be.

While shopping in the mall with my two little ones in tow, I'd have moments where it all felt too surreal. I'd think about how if I were a mom in Africa, my children wouldn't be with me as I worked, and I would not be worried about how they felt about it. They'd be in the care of a family member, and there would be no struggle or concern. Everyone would be fine. But I had no support system in the US, and I felt the absence of that often. In the US, it seemed I had to be everything to my children even though I had no personal experience to draw from. While I worked hard to be their provider, buddy, cheerleader, etc., I was dealing with the negative feelings that often came with this new concept of parenting. I can't count how many times I've watched my children playing and see them drift off into their own little world. Pretending their race car was a spaceship, they'd run around in endless little circles paying no attention to me. At that moment, they'd be so absorbed, I'm sure they didn't notice I was even in the room. I'd begin to think, *excellent, they're busy. I can get a little work done.* Next, I'm running down my to-do list in my mind when I hear, "Maaahhhhmmm… you're not watching! Look at me. Watch me do it again." Only occasionally does the African mom in me think, *I would have never told an adult to watch me!* More often, the American mom snaps her attention back, and I feel a pang of guilt for letting my mind wander to my work. This was a feeling I never imagined having to experience. So while I was learning how to run my businesses, I was also learning how to parent in ways I'd never had examples for. Even if I had the examples to follow, it still would have been nice to have my husband around to help. But that was seldom the case.

When we initially moved to the US, we only had one car to share. My husband worked 7 minutes from our house, so it made sense for us to save our money on a second. As much money as it did save, looking back, I wonder if it was worth the struggle it created as I tried to get Ansell Dresses off the ground. Nearly every day, the kids and I would have to get up in the morning with my husband around 6 a.m. While he got ready for work, I'd get the kids up, ready, and into the car to drive him there. When we got back home, we'd have breakfast, play for a bit, then I'd put them down for naps. While the kids napped, I'd take my pictures for the Ansell Dresses Facebook page and finish up some housework. When the kids were awake, we'd go back out to buy dresses, always making sure we left in time to pick up my husband from work. On the days he needed to work late, I'd have to keep the kids awake in order for us to go pick him up whenever he was ready. And if he needed the car while he was home with the kids but I had it, that was an entirely different headache.

Most days, I was doing everything by myself. Caring for the kids, managing the house, and building my business. At one point, my husband's job required him to travel about three weeks out of each month, so it would just be the kids and me doing our own thing. Whenever I wasn't shopping or taking pictures, I was packing boxes and shipping them over. There is nothing that energizes me more than building a business. The excitement of figuring out what to do and how. The rush of knowing that every minute I put in means money coming out. Starting a business was exhilarating. But it was also exhausting. What I would have given for my husband to come home early and give one child a bath. What I would have traded to wake up because I was done sleeping, and not because a child was crying or an alarm was ringing.

How much I wished someone else would change one diaper, tie one shoe, buckle one car seat. It was all me, and there was nothing to do but keep going. I was still just as ambitious as I'd been when I was younger. My goal was to make a million dollars by the time I was 25, and during that time I still had a ways to go, but I had no plans of slowing down before I got there.

## Slow Down When Things Get Crazy Before You Have To Take A Seat

Over the years, I'd learned the many ways in which opportunities could come. Some you had to create from scratch. Others might fall out of the sky and land right in front of you. While I was getting Ansell Dresses up and running, one came as a spin-off of that idea, and I realized I could work them in tandem. Like how my popcorn business led to a candle selling business when I was a child, the opportunity to acquire and sell other types of clothing in Uganda arose. I'm a firm believer in keeping your options open. Even if you have something going on that's doing well, that doesn't mean you should keep all your eggs in one basket. I had Ansell Dresses, my most lucrative business to date, but I didn't see any reason to only work on that. Pretty quickly, I realized how negatively that frame of mind could affect me.

Early on, I noticed big bins outside of convenience stores and on the sides of roads. I later learned those bins were donation boxes meant for people to drop in gently used clothing and shoes. Those items were then either donated or sold for a significantly lower price by the owner of the bins. This was usually a company or a business person who understood the specifics of sending things between the US and other countries. With further research, I learned a large percentage of the contents of those bins went to Africa. The shipments were large and frequent, and they got through successfully, intact, and within a reasonable timeframe. Understanding the systems they used to make this happen would be invaluable to my own business, so I dug a little more. I found out the bins' owners would gather all the donated clothes and put them in these massive balers that could tie together 1,000 pound bundles of clothing. They would take the finished bales and sell them to wholesale buyers for a profit, usually overseas. Other organizations would do something similar and get their clothes from a second-hand store like the Salvation Army, buying things in bulk at a significant discount when they didn't sell. Clothes acquired that way would follow the same shipping process of sending by the 1,000 pound bundle.

When I started, I would purchase the unsold clothes in 2,000 pound bales at about 10¢ to 20¢ per pound from Goodwill. I'd take them to my house where I purchased my own baler and set up shop in our three-car garage. There, I would separate the clothes into 100 pound bales by type. Once they were separated into dresses, women's tops, children's pants, and so on, I'd load the clothes into a container and store it in my basement until I was ready to ship everything to Uganda. And if I didn't sell the clothes wholesale, I was donating to the people I knew needed them the most like orphans, widows, and the elderly. I really liked this because I'd grown up having only two dresses, and now, I was in a place to change that for hundreds of other kids living in the same position. But it was still hard. I remember at one point my three-car-garage was overflowing with close to 20,000 pounds of clothing I had to unravel, sort, and bale all over again. Having to climb up, down, and all around these massive piles of blouses, jeans, and itty-bitty baby clothes to begin separating them for sale was extremely labor-intensive. Even more than I initially thought. That spin off business wasn't itself a money maker, but it did help to solve one of my biggest shipping issues with Ansell Dresses. Without an alternative to physically flying with my packages or paying the expensive shipping costs for much smaller boxes, my business would have hit its maximum capacity. I'd also realized that I could use my businesses not only to benefit myself, but to benefit countless others I didn't even know. I finally understood the value in a business beyond creating wealth. Unfortunately, this knowledge did little for my health at the time.

Ansell Dresses was hitting its stride and growing so fast, I was pushing my pace to stay ahead of it all. By the time I was almost seven months pregnant, all the long days and nights were beginning to take a toll on my body, but I never slowed down. I kept pushing through because I felt like there was no one else around who could replace me. There was no use wishing for a break because there was no window of time to take one. Both my children and my businesses needed me to show up 100% for them every day. In my mind, I was perfectly fine to keep going, but our bodies always have a way of healing themselves even when we refuse to make the effort. From time to time, I would feel lightheaded, even fainting once or twice and having to go to the ER. Each time it happened, I was advised to slow down. But what I considered slow and what the doctor meant were two different things. One time was really frightening. Of that day, I remember putting both of my children down for a nap in the afternoon then starting to walk down the stairs. Next, I woke up confused and disoriented on the landing of the stairs to the sound of my daughter screaming. I couldn't understand why I was laying on the floor when I'd just been coming downstairs from their room. Fear shot through me as I looked at the dark night sky and realized I'd been out for hours. The kids were frightened but fine. I was stiff, but no broken bones, cuts, or real pain. The baby inside me was rolling and kicking around as usual. After this scare, I did my best to take it a bit easier. But my days were so filled with things to be done that I was still moving every minute of the day. Until finally, my body said *enough*.

One morning my husband was leaving for a meeting in Brazil. While he was getting ready to leave, I remember not feeling well, but I brushed it off like I'd started getting used to doing and let him go without a word. But as the day went on, I felt worse. By the evening, I was running a fever and taking a simple breath was getting harder to do. I knew I needed to see a doctor right away, but by then it was too late. I was home alone with the kids and had no one to call. Managing to hang on through the night, when the morning came, I called over a neighbor who occasionally babysat the kids. As soon as she arrived, I drove myself to urgent care. I didn't know what I had, but I assumed the doctors would give me a prescription, send me home, and in a day or two, I'd be back on track. Imagine my surprise when they put me in an ambulance and sent me to the hospital.

When I got to the emergency room, I called the girl that was watching the kids to tell her I was going to be a bit longer, but right after, the doctors told me they wanted me to stay overnight. The girl watching the kids was only about 13 years old at the time so she couldn't keep them herself. Even if we needed her to, she couldn't stay late because it was a school night. Now the panic set in. Instead of relaxing to get better, I started calling my husband nonstop to see if he could help me find someone to get the kids. But for a while, he was still in the air and unable to receive calls. I was frighteningly sick, carrying a son whose life may be in danger, and unable to get to my other children who had no one to care for them – but me. I was utterly and completely alone. I hope for as long as I live I never feel as hopeless and isolated as I did in that hospital. It didn't matter how strong, independent, and capable I was. Without my husband and family back home in Uganda, it was times like these where I felt the most helpless. After a few hours of waiting, my husband's plane landed and I finally got to tell him everything that was going on. Immediately, he called a friend of his who came and picked up our car. Afterwards, they went back to our house to relieve the girl who was taking care of the kids and took them back to their house where they put them to bed for the night. But even with everything taken care of, I was still sitting in the ER just as anxious as when I first arrived that morning.

The person that was helping us was actually a really good friend of my husband's, and he and his wife were such nice people. I knew they both had work in the morning, so I kept thinking about how I had to get out of the ER before then so they could both make it in on time. I didn't want my issues keeping them from providing for their family. My children never left my mind. Everything that happened that day was unusual and different, and

I worried about how that was affecting them. They must have been frightened, confused, and just as worried as I was. I was always there for them, and they'd never slept away from home. I remembered how I felt to be their age, dependent, and not so secure about what was happening next. It wrenched my heart to think of my children feeling what I felt as a child. I could picture my son's little face, looking around at everything unfamiliar, trying to feel safe. I could hear my daughter asking for me, and I desperately needed to go to her. So that's when I made the decision that I would get out of the hospital. By midnight, I'd convinced the doctors to release me. Somehow, I'd pretended to feel better long enough for them to believe I was ready to be discharged, but when I left, I was no better than when I went in. I drove directly to our friend's house, so grateful to them for their help, and picked up my kids. When we got home, I couldn't even make it up the stairs. I was still in a lot of pain and completely exhausted. I couldn't draw a full breath, but I felt this immense relief. That night, the three of us slept on the living room floor with blankets. It was honestly as far as I could go.

I needed help. My son would be born in two months, and my short stay in the hospital made it clear that I couldn't do it alone. What if my husband was halfway across the world when I went into labor? We had no family and no one to help us until he could make it home. I applied for visitor's visas for my mom and sister to come and help me when I had our son, but once I found out they'd been denied, that was the straw that broke the camel's back. Before that, I hadn't been able to visit Uganda in almost a year because of my pregnancy. My mood and energy levels were so low, I was barely doing anything remotely strenuous. Every day I felt more and more run down, and the most homesick I'd ever been. If we had only chosen to live somewhere other than where we were, I wouldn't be halfway around the world and totally disconnected from anyone who could help. I pictured my life stretching into the future as it was today, and it felt bleak. The trajectory for Ansell Dresses was so positive. With the changes and improvements I'd made, and the development strategies I'd put in place, the potential was even greater than I imagined. The problem was, I couldn't commit the time to it. I knew if I wanted to build the store to what I envisioned in my mind, something in my life had to change. It was obvious I wasn't going to be able to take things as they were much longer without jeopardizing everything I'd worked for. I tried my best to stay positive. Tried to find the opportunity and advantage to turn things around just as I always had. But by the time our third child was a few months old, I wasn't myself at all anymore.

On the surface, things were going well, but I was so sad. Today, I know I was suffering from postpartum depression, but back then I thought things like that weren't real. The way I'd been raised, you didn't get sick in the head. If you had physical pain, you took some medicine and got right back to work. But I knew this was different. Once our son was born, I started feeling even more tired than I'd ever been. I was becoming detached from everything I loved as if they didn't mean the world to me. My husband was never home and because I had two toddlers and a baby to look after, it felt like I might as well have been a single mom. My work was taking up such a large amount of my time, and he was working so much I could never get any rest. When you're a parent you have to constantly think on the fly, be the bigger person, the referee, caretaker, nurse, stylist, therapist, and the list goes on and on and on. Being blessed with children suddenly blesses you with so many new hats to wear. In addition to that, I wore the hats of a wife and businesswoman just as often. Then there suddenly stopped being enough time for me to enjoy all the things I'd created for my life. But the store was growing so rapidly, it needed my undivided attention no matter how I was feeling. So when we moved to the new mall location in August of 2013, I got on a plane to Uganda for the first time in a long time to supervise the opening and help things along. I told my husband it was going to be a routine business trip. When I arrived, I pressed my son, daughter, and baby into the arms of my ecstatic family members and slept. After many hours of sleep, and many more hours of thinking, I called my husband and told him I wasn't coming home.

## When Crisis Comes, Count Your Blessings

My ultimate decision hadn't been a knee-jerk reaction to fatigue, stress, or emotion. I wasn't trying to manipulate, punish, or hurt my husband. In the months leading up to my trip to Uganda, I'd been begging him to leave his job. I knew the way we were living wasn't working out for me. I still had so much resentment built up from when we moved there in the first place. It was hard to see past that and start being happy. The job he chose was supposed to be better for our family, but my husband was working so much and traveling alone all the time, it almost felt like it was ruining it. More than anything, I was struggling and couldn't help but feel like I'd be better off alone. I didn't really have any friends or family where we were so it was really hard taking care of the kids and working from home. I kept thinking that back in Uganda at least my family was there and they could help me. Some days I just needed a break. But with my husband gone most of the time, I never got it. Plus, with the dress store becoming even more popular and me having to travel for my other ventures and investments, it didn't even feel like we were married. Somewhere down the line we'd become two people who sometimes lived in the same house and drove the same car.

When we first got married, we vowed to spend as much time as we could with each other, support one another, and travel the world together. But I thought about it and noticed we hadn't traveled anywhere as a family since we'd left Egypt. His job was taking up all of his time and motherhood and entrepreneurship were taking up mine. And I'd not been silent about my circumstances and what it was doing to us. From his vantage point, the job he chose meant more money, better paths to advancement, and excellent benefits. But he was working so much it undermined any pleasure we could possibly get from those advantages. I thought an easy solution to this problem would be for him to leave his job and find another that wasn't so demanding. He'd had plenty of offers like that before. He just didn't see it that way. To him, leaving a good job that supported a very nice lifestyle made no sense. He saw it as a loss to consider anything that required less travel and a lower salary. But to me, gaining him back in our lives would be worth every penny. Besides, the revenue from Ansell Dresses was quickly growing and could easily fill the income gap. But this was something I couldn't explain to my husband in a way he'd understand. Either that or he just didn't have the capacity to hear it. I knew that as my career flourished, I'd get even busier. So in my mind the only thing left for me to do was leave. Just like I'd done so many times before. If something I was doing wasn't working out, I let it go and waited for something better to come and replace it. However, when I arrived in Uganda, it was like my attitude changed almost instantly. I already had better. Why was I looking for it to be replaced? I thought about the picture of my future I'd held as a child, compared to the reality I now lived. So many of the things I envisioned were true, and I began to doubt my thought process. Was I being too dramatic? Ungrateful?

As I walked some of the same streets where I used to sell popcorn and candles, I couldn't help but think back to the days when I dreamt of having what I was currently running away from. I knew what real suffering was because I'd experienced it when I was a child. I'd even witnessed it into adulthood as I traveled the world with my husband. Remembering what it looked like to see an entire family stacked on top of a small motorcycle in Thailand has a way of making you think differently about having only one car in the States for yours. It's true that I was struggling, probably a side effect of my nonstop ambition, but I immediately felt like I was acting like a baby when I thought about the way I was coping with it all. As I gave pocket money that could last a month to the young girls selling whatever they could to take care of their families, my perspective shifted. Traveling through the slums, and seeing the red dust covering everything, I recalled my spotless home and clean clothing. I looked at the walls and roofs that let the water drip, seep, and rush in, and I thought of my sturdy foundation with its furnace, air conditioner, and hot running water. I saw the cramped spaces with people stuffed inside and estimated how many little shacks could fit onto my extensive property. And then I saw all the people with smiles on their faces and friendly greetings despite their difficult circumstances. I was overwhelmed. In what now seemed like another life, I'd been one of those smiling, optimistic people. I remembered that happiness still happened even in the most unlikely of places. Running myself ragged to live out the same dreams that were supposed to make me my happiest suddenly stopped making any sense.

Going back to Uganda helped me slow down and reassess. Just like how I needed to take a moment to reframe my businesses, I needed to do the same in my personal life. Staying away from what was bothering me gave me time to think about all the things I'd hoped and prayed for, everything I had to be thankful for in the present moment and what many other things I could one day add to that list. By forcing me to face all the hardships I'd left when I moved away five years before, that trip gave me a fresh outlook. It made me contemplate all the blessings I'd been able to see since then and find ways to deal with all the new, unique challenges I was now facing. The fact remained that the first reason I'd gone back home was to open the hottest new store in my hometown with my kids right there by my side, just like they'd been all along when I was building it. I really was living out a part of my dreams. But the same person who listened to and supported this wild idea of mine wasn't anywhere to be found. We should have been standing there, holding hands and smiling together, but we weren't. Instead my husband was somewhere far away, wrapped up in the same routine that was causing me all this heartache and pain.

I would be lying if I didn't admit how frightening it was to realize my only choice was to give my husband what was, essentially, an ultimatum. What if he said, "Fine! Stay there." I was prepared to accept that risk. I had a very successful business in Uganda, and I saw living there as being an advantage over living in the US. There, I could be a more hands-on manager. Grow the company, add stores, and expand my personal shopping services with luxury brands. I could easily make enough money for me, my children and my entire family to live like the elite wealthy. I would also have all the help I needed, given the large support system I had with my mother and sisters. It would free me up to cultivate better relationships with suppliers in the garment districts in New York, LA, and other major US cities. These were the opportunities I could be grateful for. What filled me with fear was the thought of losing my husband to all of it.

I knew my husband loved my children and me. He'd stayed in Cairo during a revolution, risking his own life out of fear for ours. I believed he was still that same man. But that didn't stop me from worrying. What if I told him we wouldn't be returning until he found a new job and he decided to let us slip away instead? I did not want a divorce. I did not want this separation, or any separation for that matter. What I wanted was him, in our lives every day. Ever since I was a little girl, I wanted to be a successful entrepreneur more than anything. But I also prayed that I could raise my kids in the best environment for their growth, where they knew both their parents. I also longed to be in a marriage that was an equal partnership filled with love, affection, and quality time. I desperately wanted everything to work and the thought of losing my husband stung hard. It was enough to make me reconsider my decision to stay in Uganda. Maybe I would just finish the store opening and return home to resume life as it had been. But the fact remained. My husband's job and travel schedule were causing me to lose him anyway. And if we continued as we had been, I stood to lose much more. He would be gone to me, regardless of whether I gave in, and returned, or refused to return. But I'd learned I couldn't make him leave his job. He was free to choose. So instead, I leaned on my freedom to make my own choice.

## You'll Never Make The Wrong Choice If You Choose What You Love

Hardships are inevitable. That's just a fact of life. No matter how badly we want it to disappear, that fact will always remain. But even if we can't control the things that happen to us, *we* decide how we feel about them. It's exactly what's meant when they say, 'one man's trash is another man's treasure.' It's not what it is that matters, but how you choose to look at it. The problem is, you never know how you truly feel about an experience until you go through it for yourself, and sometimes that can be very scary. Based on my goals as a little girl, I'd set myself up for a unique set of challenges that had the potential to ruin me if I wasn't able to figure them out. My life and livelihood were intertwined. Whatever decisions I made in my business affected my life and vice versa. I'd chosen a career where there was no clock to punch at the end of the day. No moments I could relax and not be the boss anymore. I'd chosen a life where I couldn't hit pause on how fast my family was growing so I could pay attention to the growth of my businesses. Daydreaming as a child, I'd adopted entrepreneurship as a way to shield myself from those things I felt had the potential to steal my control. I vowed to marry for love and make my own money so I wouldn't hold any resentment toward my husband and he wouldn't hold any power over me, but I was still feeling some kind of way over his ability to move us where he wanted and when. I said I'd always be there for my kids and not be so occupied with my own life that I was absent in theirs, but I couldn't help feeling distant every time I shifted my focus from them to my work. I even said I'd be a successful entrepreneur, but on the other side of this new separation from my husband, I realized that I had virtually no success. He was the one with the Master's degree, he made the money that paid for our half a million-dollar home, and even with the success of my ventures, none of it was nearly enough to fully replace his salary. The way things had turned out, the way I saw it, I'd surrendered all the control I spent so long working to gain.

 I didn't know exactly when it happened, yet at some point, I'd gone from feeling this immense amount of freedom to feeling like I was being suffocated by the same responsibilities I willingly chose to pile on to myself. That's why it's so interesting for me to think about the time I spent scaling Ansell Dresses to its first six-figures because back then, I had this sort of tunnel vision. The way the story reads, everything involved with building the brand went smoothly. And even though there were difficulties, I treated them like innocent challenges. Whatever issues came up, I had solutions that worked fast and follow-up ideas ready and waiting to make things better. I loved the part of my life that made me money, but if I was completely genuine with myself, I'd let that cloud my feelings concerning all the other parts of my life that didn't have anything to do with my income.

Being someone who chooses to fearlessly set goals to chase their dreams is like being a fighter in a never-ending tournament. You either win to face a newer, stronger opponent, get knocked down and lose – forced to learn how to win when you fight again – or watch from the stands. Because it takes such an unpredictable amount of time to reach any kind of success, if you don't enjoy whatever you've chosen to do, you can quickly drive yourself crazy trying to achieve all that it takes to make it happen. If I only took into account the success of my brand, then I miraculously had enough energy, time, and know-how to grow a small side hustle into a six-figure-earning business in under a year, all while barely breaking a sweat. But once I look at the full picture of my life as an entrepreneur, all of the profits I was able to earn came at the expense of everything else I cared about. This wasn't something I really noticed until I'd already started to lose my grip on them.

Once we start treating the things that should be fulfilling to us as a means to an end, it's only a matter of time before we'll be left feeling completely drained and empty. In other words, if you don't love the journey toward the reward as much as the reward itself, then you're bound to lose your way long before you ever get close to making it. It was clear I was losing sight of what I really wanted. The success of my business was important to me and sometimes, it demanded grueling 18-hour days and sleepless nights. But I never had a problem with doing what needed to be done for the well-being of my businesses because I loved it. Even when I did those things that maybe scared me a little or would cause a bit of grief, I trusted they would bring whatever solution I was looking for to keep things running strong. Even so, my kids and how they were adjusting was just as important (if not more) as my relationship with my husband and my health. I hadn't noticed, but it had been a while since I thought about what I loved and appreciated the most about those things.

With any difficulties we might face, the only way out of them is through. But it's also true that the easiest thing for us to do is turn around and run in the opposite direction. Whether taking the easy way out is the right choice or not is what usually causes us to struggle. Just as I said before, if you're a fearless goal-setter, then you're a tireless fighter. I knew who I was and how much I could win, but it was like from the moment my husband picked Pittsburgh, I was getting knocked down way more than I was used to. Each time I got back up, the more I questioned whether I should even keep fighting. *If I'm not winning, am I willing to keep learning from my mistakes? Should I just throw in the towel and take a seat?* For those of us who choose to follow our dreams and set goals for ourselves, times like these happen more often than not. Especially if you're an entrepreneur. When hard times come, it can feel like they're under a magnifying glass. When you have ownership, the wins are more monumental than if you weren't the one making all the decisions, but so are the problems. Which is why it's important to face all of them with your undivided attention. It's through those issues that we have the chance to find our best outcomes.

As I talk to more women starting out in entrepreneurship there are very few who, when faced with what I was, would choose the path I did. Typically, when a businesswoman, or any working mother and wife is faced with an inevitable struggle to balance work and home, far more often than not, she scales back at work. The instinct is to pull back on what's going well to shovel more time and effort into the thing that's failing. But that instinct isn't driven by logic or thoughtful analysis, but by emotion and fear. These emotions and fears are exactly what drives the desire to pull back. The problem with this is that it rarely addresses the root cause of why things are not working in the first place. And so, things continue to spiral downward despite your best efforts. While you continue to throw more time, effort, and attention to battle the symptoms of a problem, you take time away from the things that will help. The reason so many women fail when starting a business or a side hustle is because they follow their hearts rather than their heads. It's not easy to overcome instincts and create a mindset that puts head over heart. But it is absolutely vital for any person who wants to start and grow a business, even if it's a small side hustle. The fear of loss will drive you to mitigate rather than capitalize on risks. You'll also avoid rather than face and defeat obstacles that could grow and threaten the health of your company. Think about what would have happened in my case had I given in to fear, drew back, or taken a position to protect and preserve. First, I would have lost my business. Had I continued to steal more and more bits of my professional time to make up for what my husband was unable to give, Ansell Dresses would have failed. In addition to losing a successful business, if I decided to continue assuming the bulk of the work, I would have lost my husband. As much as emotional instinct drove me to pull back, preserve and protect, it would have caused the demise of everything.

You may not know for sure if something will turn out the way you're thinking, but life is full of choices, and there's no way around that. As long as you choose what you love, you'll never make a wrong one. With love, everything always works out. The universal rule is, whatever we think, we see. So if most of what we experience is love, then that's what we'll see the most of in our realities. For the majority of that first year I was living in the US, all I could think about was how tired and overworked I felt, which wasn't normal for me at all. The thoughts I was thinking were far from loving. I was the same girl who worked long hours and hustled her way out of Africa, but now I was becoming exhausted by all the things that used to energize me. I realized that the entire time things had been going wrong, I was manifesting them that way. Throughout my life, I'd always believed things had to be hard for me while I worked on reaching my goals. That's just how they'd always been. When I first started selling popcorn to the people around our house we had to leave the property shortly after. When I started to sell more things later into the evenings, the arguments with my mom over what time I came home happened more frequently. No matter how good I was in school, it hardly mattered because I never had enough money to attend. From not receiving my visa in London to coming to the States early, there were so many things that kept coming up where I could have chosen to give up, but I never let anything phase me. There was a time when I thought it was fun to face those kinds of challenges. But after all those years of having to think on my feet and figure things out, one day I stopped feeling like that. Once I found myself feeling like a single mother back in my home country, I was tired of having to problem-solve my way out of everything. And at that point, I recognized what I wanted most was for things to be easier than they were turning out to be. But instead of focusing on what I didn't like, this time, I turned my attention to the things about my new life that I loved. I hoped this way of thinking would bring me the essence of what I wanted, like how it used to be when I'd find a mango on a tree instead of the money to buy it.

Putting myself in those same shoes where I first found myself in the slums of Uganda, I started to think of the things I presently had in my life that brought me the most joy. I thought hard about the things I actually liked about living in Pittsburgh and how we were spending our time there. I remembered all the mornings the kids and I would drive their dad to work. Even though I would be so tired sometimes, I still enjoyed the intimate moments we got to share in the car ride over. The trip would take less than 10 minutes, but we'd still use all the time for catching up and tuning back into each other. We'd talk about work or whatever came up, like what I would be doing that day and what he might be doing that day. It became a time for us to bond without worrying about our packed schedules getting in the way.

I thought about how I'd started to notice the kids taking pride in helping me with the dress store. They'd pick out dresses and make boxes, and while they watched me and their dad navigate our careers, I could tell that they were learning the value of putting in an honest day's work. I also remembered why I was even doing most of what I was doing. I'd made specific promises to my kids before they'd even been born, and they were promises that I intended to keep. It wasn't fair for me to blame myself for taking the time to provide for them the best way I knew how, so there was no reason for me to continue attacking myself. I loved providing for them and taking care of them as a stay-at-home mom because it was like we were working together. We were both growing and learning as time went on and I loved that I got to witness that, and have a hand in it as well.

Then I imagined some of our last few vacations and how much fun we had simply spending time together as a family. Before I left Pittsburgh, I'd started to imagine a future where I lived and worked without my husband, but that was never something that made me happy. I thought good thoughts of a better future where I could host a big Christmas with everyone we knew the same way my dad did. I got excited about the new location for the store and thought more about how we could fill all the newly empty spaces. I never said, 'if I have this, then I'll be happy' because presently, that wasn't working for me. Neglecting the things I loved to do things I didn't love in the hopes of getting what I loved - it was that disconnect that had me feeling rundown. Once I focused on simply being happy, the happier I became.

Whatever it is that calls you, listen to that and follow it fearlessly. Anything you love, focus on it intently. Imagine experiencing that love every day you don't have it, believing that it'll soon end up finding you. Then you'll notice each good thing you find always leads to another. So whatever your ultimate goal is, as long as you know it will make you happy, try to feel this same way in your present moments. The smallest steps start to accumulate and lead you to what you were looking for all along.

Think real hard and ask yourself, 'What do I spend my money on?' Whether you buy clothes, or cars, or toys for your kids

– if you're spending money on anything, there's a reason why you chose it. For most of us, outside of bills and expenses, it's on the things that we love. I love being an entrepreneur. That's what I spend the most of my money on. Part of why I can grow my businesses so fast is because the moment that I make money, I'm already figuring out how it can bear fruit. *How can I triple this?* The only thing on my mind is how I can use what I already have to get more. And because I'm constantly finding new business ideas, I put however much money I need into my working model concept and that helps me think even further about how much more I can get. *With this idea, if I got $50k and put it back into this, I'm going to get the $150k that I can use for that, and then...* I'm always reinvesting in my businesses. Of course, I spend my money on other things too. I love good food. When I was growing up we could barely ever afford anything that wasn't cheap, like cornmeal. One of my favorite things to do is eat out at the best places wherever we are. The way I treat myself for working hard throughout the day is to go and have a really nice glass of wine with an even better meal.

You can also think of those things that you miss when they're no longer around. Every night I laid my head down in the slums. I missed my comfortable bed in the old house. Before we were forced to move, I never knew what it felt like to not have enough to eat. While living my new life, I didn't think about how hungry I was as much as I missed having a full belly. When I was working long hours, I missed having pocket money for snacks. I missed all the dresses I used to have when I was alternating between only two. Following those feelings led me to not miss them anymore but create new things to miss. Other things I'd never even seen before, like keeping an eye on my family while I was overseas or spending time with my husband. While I lived and worked in Uganda when I first opened my dress store, I committed myself to keeping an open and loving attitude. I continued to focus on the good things in my experience and reminisce on the lighthearted times that led me to where I currently was. I never knew exactly what would happen once I left my husband, but that was never important for me. I held on to my belief that if I kept a loving attitude and remained patient, things would eventually work themselves out. And like a miracle, three months after I'd told my husband I was staying in Uganda, he called to tell me he'd gotten a new job in Minneapolis, Minnesota. With this new position, he'd have more flexibility, which meant more time for the kids and me. That was all I needed to hear. I think I was on the plane and back in Pittsburgh in something like three days after that phone call. After we celebrated Christmas there, we all drove the three days it took to get to Minnesota. I could tell you about the difficult and emotional conversations that followed my decision to stay in Uganda. All of the anger, disbelief, tears, resentment and pain that spilled out. The hours and days of stress and anxiety we endured. But today, ultimately, none of that is relevant. When we reconciled, it was a new year and a new start.

It was a tremendous relief to leave Uganda, return home, and be back on track. My family, my career, and my marriage were realigned, and I felt on course. For about four months while living in Minneapolis, we searched for a house to buy. In the meantime, Ansell Dresses was taking off. At this point, the new store location was a hit (we were quickly approaching that $100k mark).

By then, the wholesale clothing offshoot I'd started in Pittsburgh naturally fell off. The supply, shipping, and storage all changed with our move to Minneapolis, and it was no longer profitable or sustainable. I'd liked this side hustle the most for its humanitarian impact and hoped I would eventually find another business that could bring that same value. But with how much physical labor it cost me, it didn't hurt too much for me to let it go. In its place, I set up a couple more side hustles. My shipping capabilities had vastly improved, so I began importing African spices and coffee. Throughout all of this my husband was settling into his new job which delivered on the flexibility he'd promised.

We eventually found and bought a new house, I started to travel more for the dress store and my other new businesses, and things took off and got busy again. Except this time wasn't as bad. Because I'd been able to streamline my operations and hire employees through the store, I once again felt in control. Soon after, I became pregnant with our fourth child. With my husband home most of the time and working much more reasonable hours, we were both able to achieve an equitable balance of work and life. Once again, we were finding time for each other. The birth of our son was a joyous occasion, and we had established such a workable cooperation that it was a completely different experience for both of us. For the first time in years, I felt stable, comfortable, and content. It was like a weight had been lifted off my shoulders. My routines stopped feeling like they were suffocating me, and my days weren't filled with putting out fires. Ansell Dresses had made $100k in a little under a year, I had my husband back in my life full time, and our kids were happy and healthy. Everything felt lighter and easier. Then about a month later, my husband lost his job.

## If You Wanna Keep Growing, Don't Get Too Comfortable

Growth is a positive thing. However, it can be just as difficult to experience as destruction. This can sometimes make staying stagnant seem more appealing than moving forward and doing something different to change for the better. Have you ever broken a bone? It's the perfect example of this concept. If you let it, eventually, the break will heal and the pain will be gone as if it never existed. Your bone is even stronger by then. It's more resilient and less susceptible to being overwhelmed by the same amount of stress that broke it in the first place. But if you don't go through the pain of healing the break, then the bone will never mend, essentially leaving you with discomfort that lingers and mobility that's limited. You'll be worse off than you were before. Nothing in this life comes easy. Even feeling better is hard sometimes. Nonetheless, just because it's not always the easiest thing to do doesn't mean we should avoid opportunities for improvement.

Some of our worst moments give us the best opportunities to experience the most growth. I like to think that when we're at rock bottom, the only way to go is up. But growth only happens if we choose it for ourselves and pursue it without any fear. Just because we find ourselves at the bottom doesn't mean we won't stay there. When my husband lost his job, every single second we were without his income, our expenses ate away at everything we had faster than I could replace them. In a lot of ways, I was right back at square one. But that turned out to be exactly what I needed to snap me out of the trance that kept me content with the way things were. It wasn't that my life wasn't going well before he lost his job, in fact, I was enjoying it very much. The problem was I'd spent so much time since moving back to the US just going through the motions. I wasn't daydreaming as much as I used to. I thought what I had going was good enough, so I figured there was no reason for me to plan for better or build more. But the moment I stopped allowing myself to dream bigger than what I was seeing, I stopped growing. I stopped becoming stronger. Worst of all, I'd stopped thinking about what life could throw at me. I'd started to ignore the fact that no matter how good things were going, there was always room for the unexpected to occur. And when the unexpected did occur, I had a choice to make. I was either going to stay comfortable – doing the same things that were quickly turning sour – or do whatever I needed to do to rise to the occasion and change for the better.

There's nothing entirely wrong with feeling comfortable with where you are and what you're doing with your life. It's okay to choose to remain still if that's what you want. We tend to want to be comfortable because it means there'll be no major changes we're forced to adapt to, no moving parts for us to keep our eyes on, and no adjustments to make for us to be happy or feel satisfied. It's normal to avoid the pain and hard work that often comes with growing into something different. But if what you truly want is to become faster, better, stronger, and less susceptible to loss than you've ever been, then you can never remain comfortable because it's the exact opposite of what growth is. Growth can be shaky, confusing, daunting, and is most certainly never a comfortable feeling. It takes time, patience, and a dedication to progress over perfection that sometimes can be a turbulent process full of difficult changes and challenges. Success, in and of itself, is an ever-evolving goal that requires growth. It's something that keeps changing based on whatever it is you say you want to accomplish. One day it might look like selling your first lemonade for 50¢, but then the next, it looks like selling your first lemonade business for $50k. For me, success had started to become characterized by my newfound comfort. But once we lost my husband's salary, my comfort went out the window. Then success became growing my side hustles to replace the income we lost, and give us the stability our family needed so that nothing like that could ever shake us up again.

I'm not sure what goes through other people's minds when their primary provider unexpectedly loses their ability to provide. I'm guessing it's something along the lines of fear and panic. *What will we do? Will we lose the house? Where will you find another job? How are we going to survive?* When my husband lost his job, none of those things passed through my mind. What I immediately thought instead was *why did I let down my guard?* Ansell Dresses and my smaller side hustles combined brought in a decent revenue, but the majority of our household income came from my husband's job. His income supported our home, health insurance, and all of our major expenses. Because my ventures were paying for our lifestyle costs, I was not worried we wouldn't pull through or that we'd lose everything. This was a problem I could solve. What I felt was anger at myself. Why had I gotten so complacent?

Why did I allow myself to become so dependent? I wasn't running any of my side hustles to their full potential because I didn't have to. I had a safety net, and I'd begun to accept less than what I was fully capable of. This was the second time in my life that something beyond my control threatened to uproot everything. Since that time, every step I took was to guard against that ever happening again. I knew how precarious life could be because I'd already lived through the harshest lesson possible. Yet, somewhere along the way, I'd forgotten that. Now, my own family was threatened, and it was my fault. Not because I caused it, but my complacency had left us vulnerable. I knew better than to allow something like that to happen. It was exactly the kick I needed to snap me back into action. Growing my import/export business became the center of my focus. Starting as a side hustle in Pittsburgh, in no time, I'd scaled it and earned my first million dollars. It seemed to happen so naturally and so quickly, it was almost hard to imagine what could have stopped me from hitting this milestone earlier. The way I was able to refine and grow my imports/exports business based on everything I'd learned in my life as an entrepreneur, I was now certain of my capabilities and unwilling to stop there.

Next, I shifted my focus to the growth and development of Ansell Dresses. The store was essentially thriving. All it needed was small upgrades I was sure would make a huge difference. Now that I was reasonably sure the location in the mall would work, I could begin to add other products customers might purchase while they were shopping or picking up an order. I thought back to my days selling popcorn and how I'd instinctively known to add candles, a convenience item, and individual cakes, something they didn't know they'd want until they saw it. When women came in to buy dresses, they were usually also looking for the items to match – shoes, bag and jewelry. I'd already done some research and was in the position to start buying and selling accessories, so choosing to do so was an easy decision. I knew the markup on accessories would be greater than with dresses. End of season sales and rapidly changing styles made them easy to acquire, ship, and sell at a higher profit. The accessories I eventually added gave my customers easy access to the things they were already looking for, adding a higher level of convenience we hadn't previously offered. They also had the potential to bring in new customers. These people might be shopping with their friends and family and not necessarily be looking for a dress, but realize how much they liked the purses we carried and buy one of those. At the same time, they provided me with an opportunity to upsell, incrementally increasing the average sale per customer.

Once I had a plan to diversify the products we'd be offering in-store, I began thinking of ways to upgrade and streamline our dress supply. Initially, I would buy all of my dresses at the malls near my house from mid-range department stores like Macy's and JCPenney. Basically, any women's stores in my town that had fashionable, affordable pieces were the places I most frequented. But when it was time to upgrade, I knew I needed to offer my customers greater variety. From the beginning, when I imagined the success of the store, I pictured us selling all different types of dresses. However, shopping at the same places in the mall was keeping what we sold within the same bubble and began to tarnish the brand I was cultivating. So much so that we started g to become known for more reserved styles appropriate for work and conservative events. I wanted to expand to

## Starved For Success

looks that could be worn to more eclectic occasions, and in doing so, push my clientele toward higher-end brands. If a woman had a black-tie gala to attend, I wanted her to shop at Ansell Dresses. If a woman needed a dress to impress on a first date, I wanted her to shop at Ansell Dresses. If a woman wanted to go to the club, I wanted her to find the outfit that would turn every head – at Ansell Dresses. Customers loved what we were currently offering, but I understood young professional women had more to do than just work. And for every one of my loyal customers, there were five that hadn't yet shopped with me. If I wanted their business, I needed to figure out how I was going to start catering to those women.

With some research, I found out about the various fashion districts in the US and how each one had a distinct style of product they carried, even offering different designers. I already knew that at Macy's, I could find a subtly stylish cocktail dress. But I learned that if I were to visit the fashion district in L.A., then I'd be able to find something a bit more risqué. In Miami, the styles were sexy and sultry. They had a certain confident quality to them. Like the women who wore those dresses wanted their clothes to say, "Hey! I'm here!" while they danced the night away in them. They were impossible to ignore. New York City's fashion styles were equally flashy as Miami's, but theirs had a more glamorous look. Their delicate fabrics gave them an undeniable sophistication. No matter the district, the dresses still had that unique American style that I was looking for, which was essential for my brand's continuity. But what made these dresses special, and specifically innovative for my business was that they all had distinct identities like my clients. With the new offerings I'd considered, I would be able to appeal to my existing clientele by giving them a larger variety to choose from. Additionally, I could grab the attention of new clients that were tired of seeing the same old things. Each would want and need to find their perfect look for any event. If I could succeed in offering those kinds of options, Ansell Dresses would reach a level I could have never imagined.

With my husband out of work, he jumped in wherever he could and quickly his unemployment turned out to be a major blessing. He was the perfect person to offer help, needing very little briefing or coaching with his business background. When one of us was with the kids, the other was working to help grow the businesses. He was out of work for about a year, but while he looked for a new job, I savored every moment we were getting to spend together. We went on a vacation every other month, even spending an entire one in Uganda together, as a family. I can honestly say, that year was the best year we had just being together. We were equal partners raising our children, and professionally, working in perfect alignment toward a mutual goal. And it was paying off. Soon, we were making more money with Ansell Dresses and the smaller side hustles than my husband had been making before with his job. The feeling was like nothing else. I'd forgotten how incredible it was to be the person who supports myself and others. It felt amazing to be the one who created stability.

Every hardship we face, whether it's in our lives, our careers, or both, has the potential to change us for the better. But only if we let it. The year and a half I spent scaling my dress store and adjusting to life in the US was one of the hardest things I'd had to go through at that point. But by the end of it all, I felt the best I'd ever felt. I stopped being satisfied with what I had and suddenly I was ravenous for more, as if I'd still been that starving little girl I thought I'd left behind. Kicking myself back into gear and making my first six figures showed me what I was really capable of. If I'd remained comfortable with my husband taking care of us and treating my side hustles like hobbies, then there's no telling where I'd be today.

It was tempting, at that point, to exhale. With Ansell Dresses and our smaller importing side hustles providing all the income we needed, the stress of my husband being out of work was no longer a concern. We had the option of him not finding a job at all and continuing to help me build my business. But then I remembered – life is precarious and everything could change in a minute. Ansell Dresses was a stable source for us, but what if that stability became compromised? Throughout my life, I'd always had more than one source of income at a time. Back in Uganda, if the lights didn't go out and I couldn't sell candles, I had popcorn and cakes. If something had happened to one of my home care families in London, I had the safari booking service and the waitressing job. In Cairo, it was cell phones and cakes. And with my husband's recent job loss, I was reminded again of the importance of having diversified revenue streams. With Ansell Dresses still a growing success and the import/export business bringing in huge profits, I began looking for the next venture.

## We're Never Without Difficult Times, We Just Get Better At Dealing With Them

It would be nice to say the hard times ended after that first year and a half of me moving to the US, but it would be the furthest thing from the truth. After helping me grow the side hustles for about a year, we'd moved from Minneapolis to Virginia Beach when my husband accepted a new job. Because our children were still young and not established in school, I didn't mind the idea of another move. But I did feel a touch of resentment. Because I'd built my businesses to the point I could support our whole family, I believed I'd established the right to help make decisions about where our family lived and how it would operate. But again, I found myself feeling pressured to follow, and I wondered if there would ever come a time it would be my turn to lead.

The longer we lived in Virginia, the more I thought about how much I missed Pittsburgh – the same place that had caused me so much grief before. Living in Minnesota, then Virginia, turned out to be more difficult than I thought they would be. When we lived in Pittsburgh, I'd never felt unwanted or unwelcome, but that wasn't the case in our current home or the one before it. In Minnesota, I'd experienced a number of racist microaggressions that made me feel like things were better in Egypt when I could be certain of who didn't want me around. And in my opinion, Virginia wasn't as nice to live in as Pittsburgh was. I kept thinking about one of the first times I went shopping once we moved there. I'd gotten so excited about starting my dress store that I broke out dancing in the middle of Macy's like there was no one else around. Part of me felt odd, but I was just so happy about getting started and all the possibilities I imagined that I couldn't hold it in. Then all of a sudden, this woman walks up to me and starts dancing too. And then we danced together in the middle of the store to the music playing over the department speakers as if we were old friends. Once the song was over, we went our separate ways, but that woman was so nice to me even though I was a total stranger. That's how most of the people in Pittsburgh were. They were happy, lighthearted, and left the city filled with good feelings. I missed those feelings and being there in the midst of it all.

Once again, I went down my list of things I loved to comfort me, thinking hard about what I cared for the most and what I enjoyed doing. After a while of brainstorming, the main thing that kept resurfacing was how much I loved helping the most vulnerable people and those in need. Right before we moved to Virginia, I'd befriended a woman who told me a story that nearly broke my heart. She'd known someone with mental health and intellectual disabilities who was unable to independently care for herself. When her parents grew too old to care for her, they sought help with the various social services agencies in their area. Their daughter would thrive in a community group home, but sadly there were none nearby willing to take her. When it got to the point that she had to be placed somewhere, the only option was more than an hour's drive away from her home. But she had no choice. She had to go. Although she needed help and supervision to live, she was active and social. She had friends, acquaintances, a busy schedule of things to do, and people to see in her old neighborhood. In her new home, she spent her time lonely, disconnected, and depressed. Away from everything she knew and loved, soon the move became too much for her to bear. Within months, she'd committed suicide. Her story pierced my soul. How, in a country like this, could a person die from lack of connection and love? Why wasn't there something available for her in the place she wanted to live? It hurt to think this was happening to her while I was here, living and working. It made me think had I'd known, I could have done something to help. And if this happened to her, it could be happening to someone else right now. I decided then and there that I wanted to start a human services agency. The idea appealed to me not only because it would solve a massive problem while bringing incredible value to people but also because it was in a completely different industry with a totally different revenue source as my retail store. If one ever struggled, the other would be strong.

I'd spent much of my life taking care of elders and donating my time and resources to the most vulnerable – people with disabilities, women, and children. The other group of people who held a special place in my heart were immigrants. It was concerning to think about the many people who knew no one and had no help or support in their new country. Our new country. I felt the need to protect and help them. Not just to assimilate, but to live and thrive. There were so many things I had the opportunity to do and learn with the help of my husband, like building credit and navigating the confusing maze that is immigration. Even with his help, I'd somehow gotten my green card rescinded before my first naturalization appointment where I was meant to become a US citizen. With my green card rescinded, every day I remained in the States, I risked deportation. We ended up getting everything fixed, but I'd have to wait another three years before applying for the next appointment, even after I'd already waited the same amount of time before applying in the first place. My transition could've been much, much more difficult had I not had access to legal assistance and someone on my side who was familiar with the process.

The thought of extending even the smallest gesture of kindness to someone in need overwhelmed me with gladness. What amazing things I could do for people like these if I applied my business skills to it. Taking everything I'd learned about businesses and how things were in the US, it seemed like a human services company was the best idea I'd had since my dress business. With that, I began researching, and by the time we'd moved, I'd already gotten to work. As I explored my options, I grew more and more convinced. First, the revenue source was stable and predictable, meaning it was not vulnerable in the event of a recession. In addition to that, it was in a completely different industry than my current businesses. So, if one faltered or failed because of a specific set of circumstances, the other would not be impacted. Finally, it was an opportunity to create a significant and meaningful impact for not one, but two vulnerable groups of people who were especially important to me. The business would support individuals with intellectual disabilities, allowing them to live in homes they loved, surrounded by people who accepted and cared for them. And I would make it a priority to employ people who were new to the country. We would hire people who were able to work but unable to find a job due to their language skills and inability to prove their work history. I understood how it felt to go to a country knowing no one, trying to navigate the workforce. Having done home health care and having supervised other people during my short time in London, I could offer a comprehensive training program to people with no experience. The thought of bringing these groups of people who needed one another together while developing yet another business opportunity was exhilarating. Going into it, I'd never felt more certain it would succeed. My husband, unfortunately, felt differently.

Throughout our marriage, I've always been the risk-taker in the relationship and my husband's very much remained the cautious, rational one. He'd always listen to my vision and plans, but getting him to go along with them was always a struggle. He'd show interest, ask questions, and probe me for more information and details I'd gathered through research. He'd want to know how much money was needed for startup and operations or what we stood to lose if my plans fell through. Then, he'd point out all of the reasons it would fail. I respected my husband for his views and the advice he had to offer. His role as my in-house naysayer had been something like an advantage. He often did point out things I hadn't thought through, and even if he didn't, his basic lack of confidence and general doubt always strengthened my resolve. Want to see me knock something out of the park? Then tell me I can't do it! Generally, what these conversations did was prompt me to go back and do far more research, thinking, and careful planning. I'd then return to him with something more ironclad, making the idea better off than it ever was. With his concerns addressed, my husband and I would normally push past the initial dissonance, and I'd move forward. But this particular time he would not budge.

To make matters worse, he'd received news there was a possibility he'd be assigned a new position under a four year-contract in Greece. When he told me, I was amazed. Stunned with disbelief. I couldn't even hide my disappointment. I'd been through so much adjusting to my new life in the U.S. that I wasn't ready or willing to pick up and relocate halfway around the world all over again. We had lived in two different countries to support his career. In the last three years alone, we'd settled in three separate states. And now he wanted to move us all to a different country on a different continent to continue to carry out his ambitions. I was over it. In that time, I'd built a combination of businesses that were doing so well, he didn't even need to continue working. This was something he knew as well, but still denied what I proposed, maintaining that it was a risk we were not able to take. I was used to him not thinking my ideas would work, but that wasn't the part that hurt the most. It was the fact that I was tired of compromising in favor of what was important to him when it felt like we rarely did that for me. He didn't want to see past the amount of risk involved with what I wanted to accomplish. I'd wanted so badly to start this business I'd become increasingly passionate about. And I shared that with him, along with my plans to make it all happen. I was absolutely certain that everything would work out, and when it did, it would be our most successful business yet. He didn't believe that it could be done. For whatever reason, instead of taking a chance on me, he remained completely committed to his job that kept us living out of boxes he never helped to pack or unpack. I stood at this crossroads with him once before, and I knew where each road would lead. I didn't want to revisit the one paved with pain and struggle. I wanted to avoid the stress I knew would result from failing to push down my resentment again. I couldn't continue to compromise in favor of what was important to him if there would never be a time he would do the same for me. If we tried that again, this time, I was certain it would ruin us.

We were also in an entirely different position with our children. By the time we would move to Greece, our oldest would be well into elementary school, as would his sister, and their brothers would start while we were abroad. After Greece? Who knew! We would have to be off to somewhere else, following whatever position was open at that point, regardless of where it was. As much as I believed international travel to be one of the greatest things a parent can give to their children, I also knew introducing them to other cultures, languages, and places is best done when there is a stable home to return to. The time for us to work anywhere in the world and travel freely with our kids was in the past. The years during and after Cairo were that window of opportunity. What we now needed to be doing for them, and for us, was settle down.

I knew I didn't want to start over, but that meant I had to figure out what I did want. The idea of relocation left me feeling uneasy. But at the same time, I felt the rise of my own unwavering strength when I considered my human services idea. Combined, these feelings brought forth an altogether new reaction to my husband's proposition that could only be articulated with one word: no. Just no and nothing more. I was done being the one who followed. So I informed him I would be making one last move, but it would not be to Greece. It would be back to Pittsburgh. In the time he would finish working out his contract in Virginia, I told him I would build the human services company I'd described and establish a permanent home for our children. At that point, he would have a choice. He could quit and help me run the businesses, or move on his own to wherever his job would take him. Either way, I hoped he would choose to be in Pittsburgh with the five of us. My husband had been the first to come to mind when I decided to put down roots there. If we made a permanent home anywhere, I wanted it to be in a place where he was likely to feel connected, comfortable, and happy for the long term. He'd been born and raised, even attended college there. His mother still lived there, which meant our children would have access to their grandmother and other family members on the Ansell side. For the short time we lived there when we first came to the US I liked it as well. Though difficult to adjust to, living in Pittsburgh turned out to be a period in my life where I had been my happiest. From a business perspective, it was a more ideal location, not only for my current ventures, but for the human services company I wanted to launch. From my research, Pennsylvania had, by far, greater opportunities, more support, and a better structure for would-be providers in the health and human services sector.

What followed in the months after were many, many heated arguments. My husband didn't believe starting a human services organization in Pittsburgh could work. Before, we'd been able to have these simple, civil conversations about the businesses if we needed to discuss them. We'd spent about a year working together to grow the side hustles and our communication had always been great. But this time, I couldn't seem to get the information through to him. And at the end of the day, I didn't care what he thought. He would not budge, but I stood firm. I always swore by my business plans and acted on them if they were as solid as this one, so I did it anyway. He continued working in Virginia expecting we'd be moving to Greece, and I continued growing my existing businesses while laying the groundwork for my next venture. Two years later, AMA Support Services, the same business he'd doubted so much, topped $3 million in revenue after only 18 months in operation. By the time 2020 comes to a close, our revenue will double to $6 million.

On the other side of our most challenging obstacles lie our greatest outcomes. This is a truth that can always be seen in hindsight. Once we've surpassed all of the things that could've kept us down, it's always easy for us to recognize how and when we were able to overcome them. But hindsight is not the present. And in the present, where we might have countless problems to solve, challenges to face, and failures to avoid, sometimes it can feel like those difficulties surrounding us, for the time being, might overtake us. It can begin to feel like a better idea to stop what we're doing altogether and go back to a time where our dreams played nicely in our imaginations. When we weren't actively pursuing them, and there was no blood, sweat, or tears to be given in exchange. However, feelings aren't facts. Hardships may bring us a sense of inadequacy, helplessness, or even a fear of continuation, but they can never stop any of us from reaching our dreams. Only we can do that once we decide to stop reaching.

Life can get scary, but that doesn't mean we have to be afraid to live it. My husband wasn't wrong about being cautious. There was a lot that could've gone left if my business idea didn't work out. However, there was so much more that I believed could go right. Even though I was deciding to start a business in an industry I was unfamiliar with, I wasn't afraid to fail. And even though I planned to move my family back to the same place I had run away from once before, I didn't doubt that this time I would thrive. Instead of letting the fear of the unknown control me, I trusted that whatever I needed to happen for my benefit would take place. It was the way things always happened in my past. Even if I did end up losing everything, and my husband didn't move back to Pittsburgh with me or leave his job to help me run my businesses, it would be far from the end of the world. I was sure that as long as I focused on what I loved the most, I'd still be successful, my kids would be completely fine, and I would still have plenty of people in my life who loved, supported, and appreciated me. So this time, I didn't budge. What mattered more to me was my own happiness, and I followed it like it was a flashlight in a dark forest because it never led me astray. My human services company, the new properties it needed, my new schedule, my new office, my new employees, and our new home in Pittsburgh surrounded by old friends and dear family were on the forefront. All of these things in my imagination were more real to me than my husband's fears or the difficulties I might face on the road to seeing them. Essentially, we were both dreaming. I didn't know for sure if what I was thinking about would work out, just like my husband didn't know for sure that it wouldn't. I simply chose to chase the dream that would turn out the best for me, and I never stopped chasing it until I saw it to fruition. Believing in myself was all I'd ever needed to push past the challenges I was facing. And by the time I'd earned seven-figures with a business that everyone else around said shouldn't have worked, I was certain the belief I had in myself was the ultimate key to my strength and my success.

# CHAPTER 8

# The Bigger Picture

## A lesson on staying the course and moving forward

Life doesn't get easier to live, we only get stronger as we live it. When I made my first $100k with Ansell Dresses, that gave me the motivation I needed to make ten times that amount, just like I'd spent most of my life dreaming about. But before I could make my first million, I had to start and run 15 successful businesses. And that's just the number of ideas that worked. Countless others couldn't even make it through the idea and planning stages. I've sold snacks, scraps, new and used clothing, cell phones, and safaris. I've been a travel agent, resort associate, and home health aide. I've owned a pool hall and a spare parts shop. Many times, my actions didn't outwardly look like they were getting me anywhere near what I was hoping for, but inwardly, I was left transformed, strengthened and more eager to try the next thing. No matter how rocky the road seemed to get, I always made the commitment to continue traveling. I'd learned that as long as I was clear about what I wanted, consistently followed whatever process I believed would get me to it, and remained patient until I got there, then whatever end would be for my benefit.

I say it all the time - I've literally created my life. I've worked hard, and I've done all these things so many other people have only ever talked about or imagined. There are so many women who could've been me, but they haven't been able to achieve what I have. Maybe they never had the chance to realize their potential and believe that they could do more. This is the reason why I felt it was important for me to share my story. I want people to see and believe that anything is possible. No matter what your life situation is, know that we can all achieve great things. As long as we remain dedicated to our vision, and the mission it takes to see it play out in our real lives, we can never lose.

## Start Telling A Better Story And Don't Stop Until It's Real

In hindsight, starting my human services company ended up being one of my greatest decisions. However, getting that business off the ground was incredibly difficult. From the time I received my first certificate of acknowledgement, the first step of many more, it was a full seven months before AMA Support Services was ready to start operating. During that time, it became more and more necessary to travel to Pittsburgh to meet in person with officials, submit documentation to establish the business, and find conducive homes and properties. I started to commute regularly from our home in Virginia Beach. The drive between cities was eight hours on a good day, 10 hours if weather or traffic were an issue. There were some occasions I'd had to make the trip three times in one week. Even the people I was communicating with while getting established would constantly mention how many people they'd seen try to do what I was doing and fail miserably. But I didn't even have the time to give their thoughts any attention. During these months, I continued managing Ansell Dresses, which required buying trips to the New York, Miami, and L.A. garment districts, and special order luxury brand buying for my personal shopping service clientele. My oldest children were established in school, and I coordinated travel schedules and care for the kids with my husband, who was still working in Virginia. My other business offshoots and side hustles continued, fitting into the scheme of things during any and all spare hours. The exhausting pace was one I was accustomed to, and my certainty that, despite every obstacle, I could make this endeavor successful, kept me motivated and committed.

Although I had total confidence in my skills and abilities to launch and grow AMA Support Services, I had growing concerns about the rising up-front costs. I had identified and estimated expenses I knew I would incur for a start-up through my initial research. This was the first time I put a significant amount of money into a company before revenue even started flowing. The business model had already been validated by hundreds of other providers. I felt assured and comfortable there would be no loss as long as I launched within a few months because the nature of the business, clients, and revenue source was stable. But as the months went on, the expenses increased exponentially. There were multiple costs I would not and could not have known in advance. I knew, for instance, I would need to buy or rent a house for our individuals to live in. What I did not realize until I received the list of requirements for licensing was that to be approved to open the house as a group home, there were dozens of modifications, upgrades, safety features and physical site requirements that had to be done and that came at a substantial cost. I knew insurance would be needed, but the specific requirements for everything from general liability to workman's comp were well beyond the estimates. And because we would be a new company in a surprisingly risky industry, we couldn't get as competitive with our rates as we had hoped. Employees had to be screened and vetted, and until we received guidance on the requirements, I could not have calculated the extent or the amount. Each step forward brought a new requirement with a price tag attached. Before we opened our doors to our first group home, I'd put tens of thousands of dollars into the company.

Five months into the startup work for AMA Support Services, the demands for my physical presence increased drastically. We reached a point where I needed to be there all day, almost every day. Leading up to this, I had been travelling back and forth, but the trips were getting longer and more frequent. Things were in full swing, but my husband's opinions and position had not changed. He remained steadfastly against AMA, continuing to vehemently express that it would not work. Even as I purchased houses, created the entity, vetted a handful of employees, accepted referrals, and began meeting with potential clients, he showed no signs of recognition that I was fully committed and moving full force to build a life for us in Pittsburgh. So, one day he came home from work to find a packed U-Haul in our driveway. I'd rented an apartment in Pittsburgh and was moving there to launch AMA Support Services.

I'd packed up the house like I did by myself all the other times we moved for his job, and if he didn't agree to leave with me that day, I was ready to do all the unpacking back in Pittsburgh without him. For nearly an entire year, he refused to help me, and I ended up having to confront him directly with an ultimatum. All the way up until the moment he finally agreed to see things my way, I was unsure of the outcome. But I never stopped trying to convince him in whatever ways I could. He had a story in his head that he was telling, but I believed mine was better. So, in the end, I followed my story until it came true before my husband's story could even start to materialize.

I've come to learn that all you need to achieve success in anything is a desire to do so and a deep determination to continue when things seem impossible. Most of all, you have to believe whatever you want is already yours. If something belongs to you, you'll never stop looking for it. You'll find that once you meet it, there is no confusion as to whose it is. It will seem like it was perfectly meant for you, as if it had your name on it all along. Whether it's a job, business idea, relationship, experience, or even material wealth. If you believe it's yours, then it is. Many of us following our dreams get caught up in our day-to-day lives and challenges where all signs begin pointing to stop after a bit of time. We start to believe we can't start a business because the timing isn't right, or we can't go back to school because we can't afford it. Whatever decision I made or action I took throughout my life, I never questioned whether or not I was doing the right thing. I only checked to make sure I was on the right track to getting what I wanted. There's a massive difference in energy between those two mindsets.

You can hope for something all you want, and you can write down every part of the plan known to man, but unless you believe it's yours, you'll never have it. It's not enough to have the passion to get something, you have to *know* you deserve it. Once you do, you'll be willing to lose a few times, if needed. I've lived as if I already knew I was going to get where I was going. Especially when I wasn't sure of which steps to take. I'd known that I was doing the right thing since the day I started making money. I was reassured when I added candles to sell, then cakes, scrap metal, and all the ideas that followed. Every single time I was presented with an opportunity to move closer toward my dreams, I took it.

When people would say they'd only seen others fail at what I was trying to accomplish, I thought to myself, *that's not going to be me.* To them, I would say mine would be the very first success story we'd all get to witness. And when my husband called himself being cautious, I looked at it as being stubborn and gave him the room he needed to change his mind. Looking back, I almost lost my marriage, but at the time, I didn't think that way. I honestly didn't know what would happen. I just stayed focused on what I wanted – for us to stay together and everything with my business to go well. Our lives are much more than just a set of perfect opportunities or the best decisions made at the right times. What we put out into the world is exactly what we get back. So, whenever you find yourself telling a story that doesn't benefit you, flip the script to say and feel something completely different.

I understand that you may not have had the kind of upbringing I did or the same experiences that have shaped my life into the story of success it is today. But that doesn't mean you aren't capable of bringing whatever you want the most into your own experience. Whatever it may be, just know that it's not impossible. It doesn't matter who you are or where you're from. Never use your situation as an excuse for not getting up and going out to get what you want. One of the most beautiful things about living today is that we don't all want the same things, so there's more than enough energy for all of our dreams to get fulfilled. All it takes is wanting, then it's only a matter of time before we have it.

Take the relationship between my sister and me as an example of this. We might be two people who grew up in identical circumstances, but our lives have been uniquely our own, and this includes our wants, our motivations, and our desires. My sister could have done the same things I did, if not better, but we've never shared the same dreams, and my path has never been hers. She's about a year older than me and just as smart. We have the same mom and dad, so we even look similar. Our upbringing was exactly the same, but we've never wanted the same things out of life. As our family fought, my sister was standing right there with me when we learned how some of our elders truly felt about us. She'd heard too when people that were supposed to love us called us worthless. But compared to how I felt, it was almost like she didn't even hear anything. When we were kicked out, my sister waited for our mom to take care of us when she clearly couldn't. She'd whine about being hungry while I did what I could to help feed us. When school was out, my sister wanted to play while I wanted to push forward in investing my time and resources into making more money. Today, I'm the one continuing to build an international empire that currently grosses millions of dollars annually. The only thing that put me in my current position, and not my sister, is my love for entrepreneurship and my desire to achieve worldly success.

Based on the fact that you're reading a book written by an entrepreneur who's seen success, I can believe you're doing so because you'd like to do something similar with your own life. But I also sense some of you might've found my words because you're seeking success in the form that makes the most sense for you. For all of my readers, I can assure you, whatever you get out of this book will be for your benefit as long as you believe. Whether you choose to start your first business (or your third), propose to the person you love or take a solo trip across the globe. Know that if someone has told you it's impossible to get what you want, ignore them. Even if everything around you seems to say that you cannot have, be, or do whatever it is you're thinking of, all it takes is your initial desire to get over that, and you will. You'll find yourself working your way backward, gradually asking all the *right* questions that lead you to precisely what you've been dreaming of. But be totally clear about what you want and don't give up until you see it. It's persistent people who begin taking steps toward their ultimate success at the same place where most everyone else before them quit. Therefore, most losers are just winners who quit too soon. If you have a burning desire, the distance it takes to fulfill that desire does not matter. Time does not matter. No amount of food, water, sleep, or whatever you think you might need to continue does not matter. If it does not feed the fruition of what you desire most, then that thing is irrelevant and will naturally fall off. Surrender to the uncertainties of your journey knowing full well that what is for you will be found eventually. And accept that you'll never have any control over a situation until you take some kind of action.

## Adopt A Now Or Never Attitude

Habit is the practice of persistence. When we create intentional habits for ourselves according to our dreams, they help us to continue on our journeys, whether we're motivated or not. No matter how small the steps, taking them as often and consistently as we can really makes the most impact. Any time I have an idea or feeling about something, I act on it right away. And acting on it doesn't always look the same. Sometimes it's brainstorming. Other times, it's mapping out concrete plans or saving money for startup costs. The important part is not how the action looks, but that it even happens in the first place. But let's face it. Now is not always the best time to do something we're unsure of. Times can get scary, and we may not feel ready to face them. But even if you're skeptical of starting, forget how you feel and do it scared. The only way things get done is if we do them. Simple as that. But when we're worried or someone we love is concerned for us, it can be easy to put things off until conditions are better. The only problem is, we never know if later will actually be better than now. In the midst of a pandemic where life on Earth seems to have slowed down, there are still men out there flying rockets into space and making plans for future trips. There are women finding cures to the same virus that has seemingly thrown us all into chaos. And there are people like me, sharing our secrets to abundant living to anyone who will listen and end up fulfilled in ways they never imagined. But while we're out here doing these things to better ourselves and the world we live in, you might still be stuck thinking you can't start now. Get out of your head! Don't think, just do. You can't be afraid to take a chance to make the change you've been waiting for. When it comes to fulfilling your dreams and meeting your goals, it's now or never.

There are plenty of things I've done that were either completely unexpected or totally terrifying. But even if I happened to hesitate, taking action always ended up helping me see how important it was to stop thinking and start doing. One particular memory I have is of when I started making and selling moonshine. It wasn't a side hustle I thought I'd ever have. In fact, I was only 12 or 13 at the time with no business dealing with alcohol. I'd already had a few good things going, but when the opportunity fell into my lap, I recognized it instantly and didn't waste any time getting started. I was on a two-month holiday with a few of my cousins. My mom had sent us to live and work on the property she owned in the upcountry. We were supposed to be helping tend the land, but the property was also right on the shore, where there were many docks and boats filled with local fishermen. When we lived there for that time, we had food, so that was fine. However, there were certain things we never had, like sugar or even kerosene for lamps. There were so many nights where we'd either have to go to sleep early because there was no light or stay outside by the fire and for me, that got old pretty fast. I knew a little extra cash would make life a bit better, but I had to think on my feet without my existing clientele or resources. Interestingly enough, during that school year, we'd learned how to distill moonshine. Down at the shore, many fishermen were drunkards, so putting two and two together, I said to my cousins, "Let's just sell moonshine." Back then, you could buy a 20 liter can of crude alcohol for about 10¢, so we bought five cans, distilled it, and sold it for more to the fishermen on the shore. I never really planned to go on holiday and make money, just like I didn't go out of my way to learn how to make moonshine so I could sell it. It only seemed like fate because I'd learned how to make something that the new people I was getting to know would love to buy. Instead of thinking how I shouldn't be selling moonshine because I was too young, or not from the area, or on holiday, I took advantage of what was in front of me as soon as it was presented.

 Whatever position you might find yourself in now, ask yourself, *what can this time give me?* What skills, knowledge, and resources can you use from your past to better your circumstances in the present? If it's not a pandemic but an economic depression, how can you use the day to get one step closer to your dreams, even if those dreams don't include a sick economy? And ask yourself these questions right now because right now is all you have. This moment is the only one like it you will ever have, and then another will take its place as if it never existed. If you choose to stand by watching every second, minute, hour, day, week, month, year pass by while you sit saying to yourself you want more, then that's all you'll receive. More time to think, hope, plan, and patiently wait, but never do, and ultimately, never have. Whatever time you spend thinking about doing something to get closer to your dreams instead of taking the actual steps it requires to get there is more time wasted.

As I write this, we are in the midst of a pandemic. COVID-19 is causing businesses in multiple industries to close. Millions of workers are losing their jobs, and companies are going bankrupt. Because my current business provides life-sustaining care to people with disabilities, we are permitted to remain open and operate. However, the risks in doing so are immense. My employees and the people we support are more likely to be exposed to the virus, which drives up health insurance and overtime costs in addition to the new and unanticipated expenses of paid leaves, which are required by law. There is a risk that revenue may be slow or delayed in coming, and operating costs have jumped. This is when the risks of remaining open are so high that many companies in our industry are partially closing, modifying, or scaling back. And some may not survive. I also see the time we're in as a difficult and challenging one but as an entrepreneur, I expect difficulties and challenges. And when they occur, I'm prepared to think and analyze rather than retreat and preserve. Knowing that one way or the other, this year would be a difficult one, we looked for a strategy that had potential. Furthermore, not only to help us weather the risks, but also position us to end the year in a stronger place than we started. The pandemic has created more need for us, both in people who need our services and those who need jobs. So, we followed a growth strategy. By the close of 2020, the company will have expanded by 36%, and we will finish the year with enough additional revenue to reinvest into the company for 2021, expanding benefits and other incentive offerings to my employees.

I can't help but wonder if other organizations in our industry are looking forward to the year to come as much as we are.

After I grew my human services company, I started to think about how important it is to be encouraged and feel prepared when we're doing things that are new or seem difficult. I really wanted to start speaking to women directly to help them see what they can do and the kinds of things they can have when they achieve their goals. I've never really been one to put myself out there. Honestly, it was the first time I actually felt afraid to do anything, which is funny because I've done so many things that scare so many other people. However, after getting knocked out of my comfort zone when my husband lost his job five years ago, I realized there were many women just like me. They were completely content with how their lives were even when they knew things could be better if they took a chance to do something out of the ordinary. I knew there were even more women who might've always wanted to start their own businesses but never did because they didn't believe they would succeed or have strong enough support systems. I figured I could teach and encourage them on their journeys by sharing my story. So, I became more active on social media to mentor women on how to start and run their own businesses. I created a YouTube channel to post videos each week for inspiration, ideas, and reassurance. And even though I've had people who've gotten to know me roll their eyes saying, 'We get it already, you're successful, you're only here to make money…' it's become more rewarding than I could have ever imagined.

## If You Wanna Go Far, You're Gonna Need Friends

There are some really big wins you could reach with entrepreneurship, but the road to meet them might be the toughest path you ever take. Having people by your side who can help you walk that path is of utmost importance. When I found *Shark Tank*, it was the first time in my life I didn't feel so alone. Before my dad died, I never had the opportunity to watch him work or ask him questions about how he made his money. We barely ever had time to speak, and even if we did, I was a young girl growing up in a culture that wasn't as open to dialogue between children and adults as some others were. For most of my life, I figured there was no one else who thought like me. When I saw people openly talking about their ideas and feelings related to all things business, it made me feel like I could trust how I was feeling. Seeing them express themselves so freely about money in the same way I thought about it gave me this unwavering assurance. I knew most people didn't talk like that, but if these people were, then I wasn't as crazy as I felt. I learned the majority of people that I encountered didn't see the world the same way I did, but that didn't mean I was completely alone.

The community of people you choose to surround yourself with has a much higher impact on your success than you think. We may be the only ones who can carry out the steps it takes to make it to our dreams, but we can never do it completely alone. Not only that, but social support is a crucial aspect of our overall well-being. When we have more people around us willing to help, it makes it easier for us to lean on them when we need to and persevere when times get tough. Without my loyal customers, I would have no successful side hustles. Without the support of a few key individuals, I would never have seen the shores of my American home. Without the help of some exceptional friends and family, I may have never believed in myself enough to sail past what was expected of me. And without my social media followers, I might've never recorded the process of building my dream home or had the courage or drive to even write this book to reach more people who are looking for answers. The truth is, we can do a lot of things alone. But if we ultimately want to make a significant impact and leave a lasting imprint on this world, we need more than just one person working toward that goal. It's the people around us who amplify our thoughts and prayers to the universe. They are the ones who usher in the possibilities for us to recognize the path to our dreams and provide us with the love, encouragement, and inspiration we need to continue following it. From the kids I used to storm the Kabaka's Palace with, to my sister and friend who helped me when I first started my dress business, I would not be where I am today without each and every one of them.

As an entrepreneur, my enthusiasm for networking has always been an asset I deeply value. The more people I meet, the more possibilities I'm able to see for myself, and the more opportunities I have available to me. Even though I didn't really enjoy living in Minneapolis, I still dedicated myself to meeting as many new people as I could. Through doing this, I learned how big of a Ugandan community there was in Minnesota, which gave me the idea to start importing coffee, spices, and some traditional foods from Africa. I'd buy all of these things and resell them to the Africans I was getting to know. When they purchased from me, they told their friends in other states, those friends told their friends, and so on. With their help, not only could I make a little extra money on the side, but I could also eat the Ugandan foods I was missing, and I could do it for free. That alone turned out to be my biggest profit.

It was a friend who introduced me to a farming dilemma that I'd never thought about before but have since become obsessed with innovating. In the midwest, the people raising cattle for beef were having issues with their hay baling system. To feed the cattle through the winter, the ranchers would bale hay in the summer and fall to be stored for later. However, I learned that the synthetic material they were using to wrap the hay for storage throughout the winter was harming the cows if it wasn't entirely removed before they ate it. Unfortunately, that wasn't a rare occurrence. If the cows were to ingest that wrap, they wouldn't be able to digest it. This would leave them either unable to put on as much weight as they should or dead altogether. I knew there were plants in Uganda, like plantains that could be used as a better substitute. I figured if the wrap was made of an organic material, there would be no need to remove it entirely before the cows fed, and they might be able to gain even more nutrients than before. I tried for a while to find a way to make it work, but as the technology stood, the organic material wasn't strong enough to be mechanically stretched for use without breaking, so it never worked out. But it's still something I continue to think about because I know once I come up with a lasting solution, that idea would be revolutionary for the cattle ranching industry. If it wasn't for my friend teaching me about the issue and introducing me to the problems ranchers face, this idea might have never crossed my mind. Now, however, I'm on the verge of making a major impact where I never imagined I would or even could.

With Ansell Dresses, I learned how notorious retail businesses are for their failure rate. As I was researching, I surmised there was something of a pattern to that failure. It was challenging to attract customers and keep them coming back. For example, a boutique would open online or in a retail space. At some point, there would be an initial excitement for the products and styles as shoppers discovered the brand, causing sales to spike. Many would be one-time buyers, but some would be repeat customers. Slowly, sales would drop over time as those repeat customers migrated to the next new boutique or shop. I had an advantage with Ansell Dresses because I sold US products and styles. This was not something every retailer in the area was capable of doing. But that wouldn't prevent the loss of my customers if anyone capable moved into the neighborhood. This concept enlightened me to the importance of a buyer's relationship with their suppliers.

With a simple Google search, you can find information online about wholesalers in various garment districts. You can learn what designers, brands, and styles they carry, who they'll sell to, and how to contact them if you're a buyer. If you wish, you can even establish yourself with them to the extent that you can purchase garments and other products without actually going there. But this, I learned, is where a new boutique owner goes wrong. Only by physically going there can you see the difference between what's available to you online and what's available in person. By personally visiting the wholesaler, you establish yourself as a big ticket buyer and build an important relationship with them. Through this relationship you will gain access to a larger variety, improved quality, and better prices. Now, fashion houses that are not open to the public will also be at your disposal, putting you at a considerable advantage to competitors who are only buying online. The difference between going there to shop and buying direct online is tremendous enough that it could be one of the most important factors in determining whether a retail store will succeed or fail. When I coach women who want to start online boutiques, I stress focusing time, effort, and money in physically going to a garment district in a major city or market to reap the benefits of establishing relationships. This is something I've continued to do with Ansell Dresses. There are now places in New York, L.A., and Miami where the moment I walk in, they throw everyone else out, lock the doors, and give me the run of the place. That's the power of relationships.

In addition to building and cultivating relationships with suppliers in the garment districts in New York, L.A., and Miami, I was researching and taking actions to expand into high-end and luxury brands. My personal shopping customer base had grown, and I'd established trust with customers placing special orders for the past year. I'd started taking advance payment to purchase shoes and bags from upscale brands like Chanel, Louis Vuitton, Gucci, Prada, Christian Louboutin, Yves Saint Laurent and many others. I saw potential in cultivating and building this aspect of Ansell Dresses. No other shop, boutique, or supplier offered this in Kampala, and there was a need. A small one, given the number of people who have money to afford brands like these. However, what I knew was when someone wanted a Prada bag or a pair of Chanel shoes, she would have to go somewhere outside of Uganda to get them, most often to Europe. I could offer a convenient alternative to that. So while I established relationships for clothing in the garment district, I began doing the same with the more elite brands.

These connections are what's kept Ansell Dresses thriving as it's grown to what it is today.

With the help of a friend, I finally decided to start my human services company. She was a lawyer I met who lived in Minnesota but was also originally from Uganda. Before we met, I had the idea to venture out into the healthcare industry. From what I understood of my research, I'd need certain certifications and credentials that I wasn't willing to earn. I wouldn't need to become a doctor, but the information I was coming up with told me that what I was trying to do was easier said than done for someone with a high school diploma and little college. For a while, I felt like I might have to stop trying to formulate my plan because the idea was a bust. That's when I got in touch with my friend. She and her husband both had careers in law, but they owned a healthcare company as well. Through her, I learned all the schooling I was starting to tell myself I needed was unnecessary, and it would be easier to start than I'd initially thought.

Through the people I've had the pleasure of getting to know, I've found countless things I love and enjoy. I've been able to do things I never thought of and grow in ways I didn't think I could. Even looking at the relationship between myself and my husband with all of our back and forth. Without all of those times, I most definitely would have never started my human services company. Through him, I've been able to exhibit my true power, strength and freedom. Also, without trusted colleagues, I might've never grossed millions of dollars. The first six months after opening our doors for business were very hard to navigate. Remember, I had no experience whatsoever in the healthcare field outside of my caregiving work in the past, and what I was doing then was nowhere near as complex. However, when any challenges came up, they turned out to be exactly what I needed to learn. Not being as knowledgeable from the start meant making enough mistakes in that first year to run the risk of being shut down.

## There's Always Something Else... Keep Going Anyway

AMA Support Services is a government-contracted organization. Before I started running it, I was familiar with government contracts, but not the operations – namely, paperwork. In the eyes of the State, if your records are not in order then your business is not doing well. Additionally, I'd vowed to service those individuals who had higher needs, and therefore, were the most risky to take care of. They were people who had a long, difficult time being placed and showed signs of being 'problematic' to other companies afraid of their insurance premiums rising if they helped. I wanted to help these individuals more than anything. But, I never took into account the extra paperwork we'd have to do or the extra money we'd have to invest to do so until those issues came across my desk.

For every dollar the government paid me, they sent four people to audit what we did with it. There were caseworkers, county monitors, and state oversight representatives all checking for something, asking for records, requiring proof of something, and expecting reports. When I reviewed the regulations they cited, I would respond in a way I thought was in accordance with them, only to have an auditor or caseworker later interpret them in a way I would have never guessed. I found that the industry operated according to a set of cultural norms that only the people inside it understood. For instance, if the regulation required annual furnace checks and filter cleaning – which it does – I would call a heating and cooling technician and have the checks done. But when an auditor came, they wanted to see proof it had been done. Showing the clean, new filter wasn't enough. They needed a receipt from the heating and cooling company. So, they'd issue a citation for the regulation violation. To clear the citation, I would have 30 days to provide a copy of the receipt for the furnace cleaning and create a plan to ensure the cleaning would happen every year. I had sent the receipt along with a statement assuring the cleaning would happen, and they would escalate the citation because the invoice had the company's address and not the address of the home where the work took place. Or because the heating and cooling business forgot to put a service sticker on the unit along with the date. The government would then send someone to audit each location every few months to make sure the sticker's date was within the year. Even the smallest thing seemed to have an expected action we weren't told up front, and every problem had a correct solution that we had to learn through process of elimination. The clients were loved, cared for, happy, and living their best lives. But the issues, citations, and monitoring reports kept coming because we didn't know the secret language of the industry. There was no time for me to do what I typically would do – get in there and learn just by doing it. If I couldn't bring an industry expert on board to help us navigate these issues immediately, we could lose our license and our contract.

By the end of the first year we'd cleared about $250k, but we had a lot of good reviews and referrals. So with leftover profits, I hired a management team who could lend expert knowledge and experience. I brought on a director with industry experience. She helped me assemble a group of people who understood what those of us unfamiliar with the intricacies of human services could not. Within six months, this team addressed and resolved the lingering issues and concerns, and put basic things in place to make sure regulatory requirements were met.

AMA Support Services, the human services company that wasn't supposed to work, was both the best and most difficult business venture I ever attempted. From finding the right employees to properly screening clients and securing the appropriate properties, there were so many challenges I had to face. Yet, I never once thought of stopping. It is not my biggest money maker by far, but it is the one I consider my foundation. It was the company that brought my family to permanently settle in Pittsburgh, a place where we've built lifelong connections. It was the company that taught me more about business administration than I could have ever learned through a formal education. Through it, I developed the skills of an executive, which I've used to take all of my other endeavors to another level. I've never worked harder to bring a company up. For all those reasons, and many more, it is one of the closest to my heart.

## Even If You Can't See It, Reach For It Anyway

As an entrepreneur, part of being successful is thinking about what's next and capitalizing on what you believe to be inevitable. After spending so many years striving for monetary success and capitalizing on those opportunities, I'm now viewing things a bit differently. My journey began with my will to prove to my family that I was not worthless, but my ultimate desire has always been to help others. It was the reason why I started selling candles – my neighbors said they needed them. It's the same reason behind why I founded my human services company – to help individuals who have the toughest time getting the care they need. My hope is, whatever I can do to make other people feel safe, happy, healthy, and strong, I'll do it. Because when we are full of these feelings, there is nothing we can't achieve.

I still dream. My family and I are building our dream home as I write this today. Three years ago, I would find myself caught in my daydreams, visualizing the perfect piece of property I have now. I look at my YouTube channel where I currently have a little over 7,000 subscribers, and I think about how I can't wait to get to 100,000. Sometimes, I don't even realize when I'm visualizing and manifesting because it's become a habit for me. Some people make a new vision board every so often, but I obsess over what takes place in my imagination. I still work at my own pace and race my own race. I don't look at what other people are doing or how fast or slow they might be going relative to myself. How other people are doing is none of my business unless it helps me and/or them.

Remember, every single thing achievable today was only changed from the impossible when someone made an effort to see and do something different. My plans for the future are to continue expanding and strengthening my platform to better help those in need of the specific types of support that I'm able to offer. I plan to conquer the State of Pennsylvania first, then take on whatever other states need transforming. Working with the individuals I've begun to work with through AMA has really opened my eyes to how much the word *inclusion* is thrown around but very seldom demonstrated. I've had to learn that accessibility does not equate to availability, and that's a problem. Seeing my clients have almost no way of staying quiet in a public library due to their disabilities makes me want to build libraries for them to feel included instead of singled out. Seeing the state of immigrant populations in the US today makes me want to fight harder to help those who are new to the country. Ideally, they should be able to grow and love it the same way I did, and pursue the same kinds of opportunities myself and countless others have. Hearing the news of riots erupting all over the country and parts of the globe in response to the Black Lives Matter movement pushes me, even more, to do what I can to shape a better world for my kids to grow up in. I've never been 100% sure of what I could accomplish. I'm not superhuman. I don't have a crystal ball that tells me which choices to make or what decisions are the best. I like creating routines and building business plans based on reliable research, but that doesn't mean I have all of the answers. All I do, and all I've done since I was 10 years old, is use my imagination to formulate the things I want to see in my reality. And I worked as long and hard as needed to make those things happen.

I am a dirt poor girl from the slums of Uganda who grew up to be a 30-year-old multi-millionaire. I was born the wrong gender, in the wrong place, to the wrong set of circumstances, yet here I am. I had no money, no connections, no advanced education, no advantages of any sort. But look at what I've accomplished. I did all of this from nothing.

So what's your excuse?

If you want to see a brighter future for yourself, then all you have to do is go after it. Use this moment to envision what can be and take bold, decisive action toward it. There is absolutely nothing stopping you. Even when there are no signs for achievement, you have to see past the lack of their existence and into the abundance of possibilities that have the potential to arise. Whatever you believe your limitations or barriers are, stay focused and diligent, and move over, around, or through them. Understand that the actual sky is not the limit. You are. Don't overthink anything. Keep things as simple as possible. Start immediately and finish as fast as you can. And never take for granted the people, places, things, or experiences you've been able to encounter. By leaning on these lessons, you will build resilience that allows you to take on any challenge. No matter what your life situation is, you can change it. Trust yourself to follow through and you'll do amazing things. Believe you're capable of seeing everything you dream of, and soon you'll be living there. And always stay hungry, starving, for more.

# About Author

Olivia Ansell is the founder and owner of Ansell Dresses, a Facebook-based marketplace turned elegant storefront currently located in Kampala, Uganda. She is also the founder and owner of AMA Support Services, a healthcare-based company located in Pittsburgh, Pennsylvania, catering to individuals with developmental disabilities. Ansell was born in the Republic of Uganda, forced by tragedy to adopt the entrepreneurial mindset that has helped her survive a challenging adolescence and grow to build the multi-million dollar grossing businesses she now owns today. Ansell is also currently doing the work to bring clean water to African countries through a budding non-profit organization meant to distribute critical filter technologies across the continent. She is married and the mother of four children.

www.ingramcontent.com/pod-product-compliance
Lightning Source LLC
Chambersburg PA
CBHW051703160426
43209CB00004B/1002